DATE DUE

Dedicated
to my beloved children
Bruce, Charles, James and Lucinda

Pedro Menéndez de Avilés

Pedro Menéndez de Avilés, founder of St. Augustine, is shown here in the first publication in color of this family portrait, by permission of his descendant, the Conde de Revilla Gigedo of Avilés, Spain. The artist and the date of the painting are not known, but the family know it to be very old. An engraving which closely resembles the old painting was first published in *Retratos de los Españoles Ilustres con un Epítome de sus Vidas* (Madrid, Imprenta Real, 1791). It is recorded that Titian once painted a picture of Menéndez and that Philip II had a portrait of him, but it is not known whether these were the same.

The 1791 engraving was done by Franco de Paula Marte from a drawing by Josef Camarón. It has frequently been reproduced, notably in Ruidíaz *La Florida,* in which book it is said that there was once a portrait by Titian in the possession of the first Duke of Almodóvar del Rio. Ruidíaz also cites Pezuelo to the effect that a good engraving was made by Coello after an ancient painting owned by Doña Ana Antonia Suárez de Góngora, wife of the ninth adelantado of Florida. The present owners of the oil painting do not believe it to be by Titian and if Philip II owned the Titian portrait, it almost surely was consumed by fire in El Pardo palace in 1604.

Settlement of Florida

Compiled by

Charles E. Bennett

1968

University of Florida Press

Designed by
Stanley D. Harris

MANUFACTURED FOR THE PUBLISHER BY
BREVARD GRAPHICS, INCORPORATED, MELBOURNE, FLORIDA
THE MILLER PRESS, JACKSONVILLE, FLORIDA
DOBBS BROTHERS LIBRARY BINDING COMPANY, INCORPORATED
HIALEAH, FLORIDA

Acknowledgments

THE INSPIRATION for me to begin this field of study came from Carita Doggett Corse and the late T. Frederick Davis, both historians of note. Everyone interested in Florida history owes a great debt to the late Jeannette Thurber Connor, and the text of her work on Dominique de Gourgues, which is first published in this book, is another milestone in her illustrious path as a Florida historian without superior.

Members of the staff of the Library of Congress were of great help to me, such as David C. Mearns, chief of the Manuscripts Division; Frederick Goff, chief of the Rare Books Division; and Andrew Modelski, of the Maps Division. Albert Manucy, a historian of the National Park Service, gave me assistance in obtaining rare materials, as did Salomé Mandel of Paris, France.

My deepest debt for aid in the preparation of this material is owed to the late Dr. Rembert W. Patrick, then Graduate Research Professor of Florida History at the University of Florida. He went over every word of the manuscript and added greatly to its readability and flavor.

Finally, the University of Florida Press and I gratefully acknowledge that the aid of Mr. James E. Davis and the Elsworth Davis Family Foundation made this book possible. They generously underwrote the publication of the book and financed the color reproductions.

Charles E. Bennett

Contents

Introduction xi

Part 1
The Engravings of Le Moyne 1-87

Part 2
The Narrative of Le Moyne 89

Part 3
The Letters 123
  Philip II to Don Luis Velasco 127
  Charles IX to M. de Jarnac 129
  Letters from the Spanish Embassy 130
    May 1, 1563 131
    June 19, 1563 132
    June 26, 1563 134
    October 1, 1565 136
    October 8, 1565 137
    October 22, 1565 138

    November 5, 1565 140
    April 6, 1566 142
    May 18, 1566 144
  Letters from Menéndez 146
    To Philip II 148
    To a Jesuit Friend 156
    To Philip II 161
  Letter from Catherine de Medici 178

Part 4
The Revenge of Captain Gourgues 183
  The Connor Biography 186
  The Recapture of Florida 202

The Appendixes 229
  The Menéndez Will 231
  The Governors of Florida 241

Index 247

Introduction

THE APPEARANCE OF MAN on the continent of North America was a comparatively recent event. The Proconsul man lived on our planet twenty-five million years ago. He was followed by Zinjanthropus, who lived twenty-three million years later but could not speak because his narrow jaws allowed no free movement of his tongue. Also living two million years ago was the luckier *Homo habilis,* who could speak and develop useful habits. *Homo habilis* is believed to be the earliest known direct ancestor of modern man *(Homo sapiens).*[1] Twenty-five thousand or more years before Christ, Asiatic tribesmen probably crossed a land bridge from the Orient to Alaska. Descendants of these people spread throughout North America and were called Indians by the Spanish discoverers of the New World.

Authentic discovery and meaningful settlement of North America by Europeans came late in the fifteenth century. There are legends of individuals making their way from Europe to America, notably St. Brendan, an Irish monk, in the sixth century, and Madoc, a Welsh prince, in the twelfth; but regardless of the authenticity of these legends, neither visible evidence nor documentary proof of their visits exists. At the beginning of the eleventh century, the Vikings sailed to the northeastern shores of North America. Their temporary colonies disappeared centuries before Christopher Columbus discovered America in 1492. Columbus and his contemporaries founded colonies in the Caribbean Islands, South America, Central America, and Mexico; but north and east of the Rio Grande exploratory expeditions greatly outnumbered attempts to settle in the first half of the sixteenth century.

The precise number of European efforts to settle areas now within the territorial limits of the United States prior to the settlement of St. Augustine is difficult to determine. Even use of the best sources available will leave the serious student with questions as to the primary purpose of many Spanish expeditions. There were expeditions whose purposes were exploration, finding precious metals, or converting the Indians. Among the least known of the latter was the missionary effort led by Father Luis Cáncer and his martyrdom near Tampa Bay in 1549. The Negro slave, Estavanico, headed a scouting expedition into present-day New Mexico in 1539 and was killed on the outskirts of Cibola, the fabled city of gold. Better known than these two were the expeditions of Pánfilo de Narváez (1528), Hernando de Soto (1539-1542), and Francisco Coronado (1540). If settlers are defined as individuals motivated by a primary desire to establish new homes, none of these men would qualify as colonists, for their main purposes were exploration and discovery of gold.

From 1520 to 1564 there were four real efforts to settle areas now lying within the United States. These attempts were significant and worthy introductions to La Caroline in 1564 and St. Augustine in 1565, the beginnings of our country's permanent settlement by Europeans.

The first of these was led by Juan Ponce de León who had discovered Florida in 1513. In 1521 he loaded his ships with seed and with agricultural equipment to give his colonists the means of production. In addition to founding a colony, Ponce planned on determining whether Florida was an island or part of a continent.[2] At San Carlos Bay on the lower Gulf Coast of Florida, perhaps today's Charlotte Harbor, he fought a savage battle with the Calusa Indians. Severely wounded in the thigh, Ponce de León sailed back to Cuba where he died. He and his colonists had spent almost four months in searching for a suitable site for settlement.

In 1526 Lucas Vásquez de Ayllón, a justice of Santo Domingo, assembled 500 people including a number of Negro slaves. His colonizing expedition sailed north along the Atlantic Coast. Perhaps he landed near the Cape Fear River or the Chesapeake Bay to build homes for his settlers. The hostility of and rebellion by the slaves terminated the colony within two months.³ The disillusioned settlers constructed a boat and sailed for home, bearing the corpse of their leader. Their ship was lost at sea and only 150 survivors returned to Santo Domingo.⁴

The third settlement during this period lasted two years and earned for Pensacola, Florida, credit for being the first substantial colonization attempt within the present territorial limits of the United States. In 1559 Tristán de Luna y Arellano led a large colonization party backed by the king of Spain, the viceroy of New Spain, the governor of Cuba, and officials of the Catholic Church. The hopes of the 1,500 colonists and soldiers who sailed into Pensacola Bay were frustrated on their arrival by a hurricane. Although most of their supplies were destroyed, the settlers endured the hardships of living for two years in a wilderness inhabited by unfriendly Indians. Dissension among the colonial leaders resulted in the replacement of Tristán and the abandonment of the settlement.

After many exploratory expeditions and three attempts to colonize the area, Spain seems to have decided, at least tentatively, that the region north and east of the Rio Grande, then known as Florida, was unsuited for settlement. Philip II ordered the viceroy of New Spain to report on the wisdom of abandoning attempts to settle the country. The king's order is included here. If a royal decree positively prohibiting settlement was ever issued, it has not been found; but a council meeting which was held in Mexico pursuant to Philip's order of 1561 agreed, and so reported in March, 1562, that the order was in fact based on accurate information.

Perhaps this Spanish indecision set the stage for the entry of France into the field of colonization and territorial expansion. The French were anxious to enlarge their territorial holdings, increase their commerce, find precious metals, and have ready access for attack on Spanish treasury ships en route homeward from the New World. Hopefully, a colony mainly for French Huguenots might lessen religious and political strife within France.

Catherine de Medici, a Catholic and the mother of young Charles IX of France, followed the advice of her Protestant secretary of the navy Admiral Gaspard de Coligny. In 1562 a French expedition sailed from Havre-de-Grâce bound for Florida under command of Jean Ribault, assisted by René de Laudonnière. These distinguished Huguenot naval officers discovered the St. Johns River on May 1, 1562, and christened it the River of May. On its south bank they erected a stone column, located at what is now the United States Naval Station, Mayport, Florida. Then the Frenchmen sailed north to present-day Parris Island, South Carolina. On the island they placed another column to designate French ownership, established Charlesfort, and left thirty men to hold it as a base for a larger colony in the future. The unsupported settlement was soon abandoned, and the men who started out for France in a primitive craft without adequate food supplies suffered through one of history's most terrible voyages. Frenchmen were reduced to cannibalism. Laudonnière described these events in considerable detail in his *Notable History of Florida.*

When the civil war in France prevented Ribault from returning to his Charlesfort colony, he sought help from Elizabeth I of England. After cooler consideration of the indirect aid promised by courtiers close to the Protestant English queen, Ribault attempted to escape from England. He was captured and imprisoned in the Tower of London. His incarceration saved him; for Thomas Stukeley, his English partner, had arranged with Spanish agents to kill Ribault by sinking the ships supplied to him by the British.

Meanwhile a temporary peace in France enabled Catherine and Coligny to send Laudonnière on another expedition. In 1564 he established La Caroline on the south bank of the St. Johns River. This French colony presaged the founding of the first permanent settlement in what is now the United States. Seeing his country's commerce threatened by the existence of the French at Fort Caroline, Philip II sent Pedro Menéndez de Avilés to attack Laudonnière and found a Spanish colony. The Spaniard captured Fort Caroline and established St. Augustine, the oldest city in the United States.

Ribault arrived to take command of La Caroline before Menéndez' successful attack. The French admiral, however, ran into a hurricane and was marooned south of St. Augustine. Along with most of his men, he was captured and killed by Menéndez. Laudonnière, Le Moyne, and others escaped from La Caroline and returned to Europe.

The first part of this book contains the narrative and artistic record of one of the most distinguished of the French colonists, Jacques le Moyne, the official mapmaker of Fort Caroline. One copy of his work *Brevis Narratio* (published by de Bry at Frankfort in 1591) was colored by an unidentified artist for presentation in 1595 to Prince Maurice of Orange-Nassau. Maurice was the son of William the Silent and fought like his father against the Spanish domination in the Netherlands. This old volume is now in the possession of the Bibliothèque de Service Hydrographique de la Marine, Paris. Its colored pictures were reproduced in a limited edition by Charles de la Roncière, *La Floride française* (Paris, Editions Nationales, 1928), a copy of which is in the rare-book collection of the Library of Congress. Salomé Mandel, a French journalist and historian, went to see the Prince Maurice copy in Paris to insure that the colors used here and taken from the La Roncière book accurately reflect the original colors. She affirms that the coloring is accurate.

Although France was predominately Catholic, national pride demanded revenge for the destruction of La Caroline and the massacre of Ribault's men at Matanzas. Catherine of France favored a Catholic to avenge French honor because the religion of the avenger might quiet any protest from Philip II of Spain, her son-in-law. Some historians believe that Dominique de Gourgues was not active in the church, but he was a nominal Catholic. The narrative of his successful attack on San Mateo and the welcome on his return to France was translated by the late Jeannette Thurber Connor and is here published in English for the first time.

This collection of documents entitled *Settlement of Florida*, could have borne other titles. It might have been called "The Beginning of the Permanent Settlement of What is Now the United

States," because the permanent settlement of our country began at La Caroline in 1564 and St. Augustine in 1565. The field of inquiry was limited to the first permanent settlement within the territorial limits of the United States—therefore, the unsuccessful efforts by France in Canada and those of England on the Carolina coast in the sixteenth century are ignored. Furthermore, by choice, the materials selected and used dwell on La Caroline to emphasize the role of the French Protestant colony in bringing about the settlement of St. Augustine. Some of the writings used in this book are dated later than the period 1564-1565, the account of Dominique de Gourgues for example, but all of the material relates to the early and short period.

Modern Americans may find it difficult to understand the sacrifices and hardships of their sixteenth-century forebears. But hardship and sacrifice formed the fountainhead of our rich heritage. For this reason, they are worthy of study and contemplation. No man who gives his life to support a worthwhile principle should be ignored by history. A reading of the conflicts and endeavors of sixteenth-century pioneers should cause the modern American to rededicate his life to just principles.

NOTES

1. L. S. B. Leakey, "Man's Beginnings," *The World Book Year Book, 1965,* pp. 108-22; and Melvin M. Payne, "The Leakeys of Africa, Family in Search of Prehistoric Man," *National Geographic* (February, 1965), Vol. 127, No. 2, pp. 194-231.

2. Henry Harrisse, *Discovery of North America* (Amsterdam, 1961), pp. 158-62.

3. Harold Lamb, *New Found World* (New York, 1955), pp. 105-6.

4. *Ibid.,* p. 106; Harrisse, p. 213.

The Engravings of
Jacques le Moyne

THE MAP OF FLORIDA

Jacques le Moyne was the official cartographer of the French expedition, and this is his map of the area the French called Florida. The artist of course visited only the area of the lower St. Johns River, and in that area the map is accurate. The rest of the map he based on reports and hearsay, and it shows his conception of the North American continent to the area of the Great Lakes.

FLORIDAE AMERICAE PROVINCIAE
Recens & exactissima descriptio
Auctore Iacobo le Moyne cui co
gnomen de Morgues, Qui Laudo
nierum, Altera Gallorum in eam
Prouinciam Nauigatione comitat
est, Atque adhibitis aliquot militibus
Ob pericula, Regionis illius interi
ora & Maritima diligentissime
Lustrauit, & Exactissime dimensus
est, Obseruata etiam singulorum
Fluminum inter se distantia, ut ipse
met redux Carolo IX Galliarum
Regi, demonstrauit.

FLORIDA PROVINCIA
AB INDIGENIS DICTA IACNAZA

Mexicani Sinus pars

SEPTENTRIO

OCCIDENS · ORIENS

MERIDIES

Pars Maris Antillarum.

Cuba insula.

The Promontory of Florida, at which the French touched; named by them the French Promontory

The French, on their first voyage to Florida, touched at a headland, not very high, as the coast in that vicinity is level, but heavily wooded with very lofty trees. This their commander named French Cape [Promontorium Gallicum] in honor of France. It is about thirty degrees from the equator. Coasting thence to the northward, they discovered a broad and beautiful river, at whose mouth they cast anchor in order to examine it more in detail next day. Laudonnière, in his second voyage, called this stream the River of Dolphins, because, when he touched there, a great many dolphins were seen in it. On landing on the shore of this river, our men saw many Indians, who came on purpose to give them a most kind and friendly reception, as their actions proved; for some of them gave their own skin-garments to the commander, and promised to point out to him their chief, who did not rise up, but remained sitting on boughs of laurel and palm which had been spread for him. He gave our commander a large skin, decorated all over with pictures of various kinds of wild animals drawn after the life.

F. Delfinum

Prom. Gallicum

5

The French sail to the River of May

Re-embarking, they sailed to another place; and, before landing again, were received with salutations by another crowd of Indians, some of whom waded into the water up to their shoulders, offering the visitors little baskets full of maize and of white and red mulberries, while others offered to help them in going on shore. Having landed, they saw the chief, who was accompanied by two sons, and a company of Indians armed with bows and quivers full of arrows. After an exchange of salutations, our men went on into the woods, in hopes to discover many wonderful things. They found nothing, however, except trees bearing white and red mulberries, on the boughs of which were numerous silkworms. They named this river the River of May, because they sighted it on the first day of that month.

F. Maiſ

Leaving the River of May, the French
DISCOVER TWO OTHER RIVERS

A little afterwards they went on board again, hoisted anchors, and sailed farther on along the coast, until they entered a beautiful river, which the commander himself chose to explore in company with the chief of that vicinity and some of the natives, and which he named the Seine because it was very like the River Seine in France. It is about fourteen leagues from the River of May. Returning to the ships, they sailed still farther north; but, before going far, they discovered another fine river, and sent two boats to explore it. In it they discovered an island, whose chief was no less friendly than the others. This river they named the Aine. It is six miles from the Seine.

F. Axona Iraeana.

Sailing hence, about six miles farther on they discovered another river, which was called the Loire; and subsequently five others, named the Charente, Garonne, Gironde, Beautiful [Bellus], and Great, respectively. Having carefully explored all these, and having discovered along these nine rivers, within the space of less than sixty miles, many singular things, but still not being contented, they proceeded still farther north, until they arrived at the River Jordan, which is almost the most beautiful river of the whole of this northern region.

Resuming their voyage as before, they discovered a river which they called Bellevue [Conspectu bellum, "beautiful to see"?]; and, after sailing three or four miles farther, they were informed that not far off was another river, surpassing all the rest in size and beauty. When they had reached this, they found it so magnificent and great a stream that they named it Port Royal. Here they took in sail, and came to anchor in ten fathoms. The commander, on landing with some soldiers, found the country very beautiful, as it was well wooded with oak, cedar, and other trees. As they went on through the woods, they saw Indian peacocks, or turkeys, flying past, and deer going by. The mouth of this river is three French leagues, or miles, wide, and is divided into two arms, one turning to the west, the other to the north.

This latter is thought by some to connect with the Jordan; the other returns to the sea, as residents there have ascertained. These two branches are two full miles wide, and midway between them is an island whose point looks toward the mouth of the river. Shortly after, embarking again, they entered the arm making to the northward, in order to examine its advantages; and, after proceeding about twelve miles, they saw a company of Indians, who, on perceiving the boats, immediately took to flight, leaving a lynx's whelp which they were roasting; from which circumstance the place was called Lynx Point. On going still farther, they came to another branch of the river, coming in from the east, up which the commander determined to go, leaving the main channel.

Prom. Lupi.

13

The French commander erects a column
with the arms of the king of France

The commander having, however, returned to his ships, and having remained on board one night, ordered into one of the boats a landmark carved in the form of a column, and having cut upon it the arms of the king of France, which was directed to be set up in some particularly pleasant spot. Such they found at a point about three miles to the west, where they discovered a small creek, which they entered, and, after following it for a time, found that it came out into the main stream again, thus forming a small island. The commander directed the column to be erected on a small open mound in this place. After this they saw two deer of great size in comparison with any they had seen before, and which they could easily have killed with their arquebuses, had not the commander, admiring their large size, forbidden it. Before returning to the boat, they named this small island Libourne. Embarking again, they explored another island not far from the former; but finding upon it nothing except some very lofty cedars, larger than any they had yet seen in the country, they called it Cedar Island, and then returned to the ships. The small island on which the column was erected is marked F in the plate.

The French left in Fort Charles suffer
from scarcity of provisions

Not long after the departure of Ribaud from Florida, the men whom he left in Fort Charles (the work erected by him on an island on a stream entering the greater channel of Port Royal from the north) began to find their provisions fail them. After consulting upon the best way of meeting the difficulty, they concluded that the wisest plan was to apply to the chief Ouadé and to his brother Couëxis. Those who were sent on this business went in Indian canoes by the inland waters, and at a distance of some ten miles discovered a large and beautiful river of fresh water, in which they saw numerous crocodiles, much larger than those of the Nile. The banks of this stream were wooded with lofty cypresses. After a short delay here, they went on to the chief Ouadé; and, being received by him in the most friendly manner, they laid before him the object of their journey, and prayed him not to desert them in such a strait. Upon hearing this, the chief sent messengers to his brother Couëxis after maize and beans. The latter responded promptly; for next morning very early the messengers came back with the provisions, which the chief ordered on board the canoe. The French, very happy at this liberality of the chief's, would have taken leave of him; but this he would not permit, keeping them with him, and entertaining them hospitably for that day. Next morning he showed them his fields of millet, or maize, and intimated that they should not want for food as long as that millet existed. Being now dismissed by the king, they returned by the way they had come.

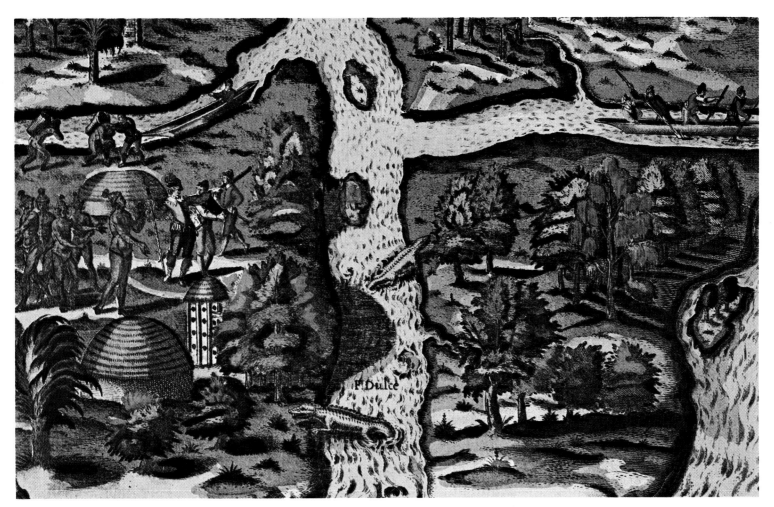

F.Dulce

THE NATIVES OF FLORIDA WORSHIP THE COLUMN
ERECTED BY THE COMMANDER ON HIS FIRST VOYAGE

When the French landed in Florida on their second voyage under Laudonnière, that leader went on shore with five and twenty arquebusiers, after obtaining a safe-conduct from the Indians, who had gathered in crowds to see them. The chief Athore, who lived four or five miles from the seashore, also came; and after an exchange of presents had been made, accompanied by demonstrations of all manner of kind feeling, the chief gave them to understand that he wished to show them something remarkable, and that he desired they would go with him for that purpose. To this consent was given; although, as the chief had with him a great number of his people, caution and circumspection were used. He then conducted them directly to the island where Ribaud had set up on a mound a stone column ornamented with the arms of the king of France. On approaching, they found that these Indians were worshipping this stone as an idol; and the chief himself, having saluted it with signs of reverence such as his subjects were in the habit of showing to himself, kissed it. His men followed his example, and we were invited to do the same. Before the monument there lay various offerings of the fruits, and edible or medicinal roots, growing thereabouts; vessels of perfumed oils; a bow, and arrows; and it was wreathed around from top to bottom with flowers of all sorts, and boughs of the trees esteemed choicest. After witnessing these ceremonies of these poor savages, our men returned to their companions, and set about choosing a place for erecting a fort. This chief, Athore, is very handsome, prudent, honorable, strong, and of very great stature, being more than half a foot taller than the tallest of our men; and his bearing was marked by a modest gravity, which had a strikingly majestic effect. He had married his mother, and had by her a number of sons and daughters, whom he showed to us, striking his thigh as he did so. After this marriage, his father Saturioua lived with her no longer.

19

After exploring many of the rivers in that country, it was finally decided that the River of May was the best one for an establishment, because millet and breadstuffs were most abundant there, besides the gold and silver that had been discovered there on the first voyage. They therefore sailed for that river; and, after ascending it to the neighborhood of a certain mountain, they selected a place more fit for the site of their fort than any previously observed. Next day, as soon as it was light, after offering prayers to God, and giving thanks for their prosperous coming into the province, they all went briskly to work; and, after a triangular outline had been measured out, they all began,—some to dig in the earth, some to make fascines of brushwood, some to put up the wall. Every man was briskly engaged with spade, saw, axe, or some other tool; and so diligent were they that the work went rapidly forward.

21

Thus was erected a triangular work, afterwards named Carolina. The base of the triangle, looking westward, was defended only by a small ditch, and a wall of sods nine feet high. The side next the river was built up with planks and fascines. On the southern side was a building after the fashion of a citadel, which was for a granary to hold their provisions. The whole was of fascines and earth, except the upper part of the wall for two or three feet, which was of sods. In the middle of the fort was a roomy open space eighteen yards long, and as many wide. Midway on the southern side of this space were the soldiers' quarters; and on the north side was a building which was higher than it should have been, and was in consequence blown over by the wind a little afterwards. Experience thus taught us that in this country, where the winds are so furious, houses must be built low. There was also another open space, pretty large, one side of which was closed in by the granary above mentioned, while on another side stood the residence of Laudonnière, looking out upon the river, and with a piazza all round it. The principal door of this opened upon the larger open space; and the rear door, upon the river. At a safe distance from the works, an oven was erected; for, as the houses were roofed with palm-branches, they would very easily have caught fire.

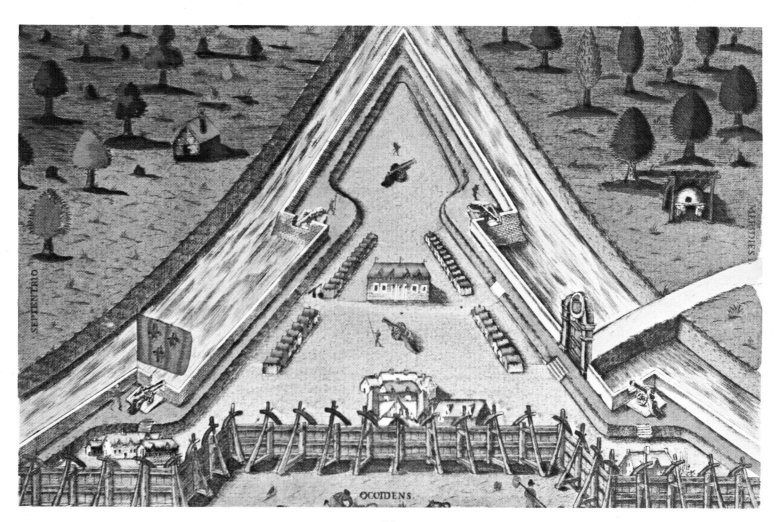

SEPTENTRIO

MERIDIES

OCCIDENS

23

CEREMONIES PERFORMED BY SATURIOUA BEFORE
GOING ON AN EXPEDITION AGAINST THE ENEMY

It is mentioned in the account of the second voyages that the French made a treaty of friendship with a powerful chief of the vicinity, named Saturioua, with agreement that they were to erect a fort in his territory, and were to be friends to his friends, and enemies to his enemies; and, further, that on occasion they should furnish him some arquebusiers. About three months afterwards, he sent messengers to Laudonnière to ask for the arquebusiers according to the treaty, as he was about to make war upon his enemies. Laudonnière, however, sent to him Capt. La Caille with some men, to inform him courteously that he could not just then supply any soldiers, for the reason that he hoped to be able to make peace between the parties. But the chief was indignant at this reply, as he could not now put off his expedition, having got his provisions ready, and summoned the neighboring chiefs to his aid; and he therefore prepared to set out at once. He assembled his men, decorated, after the Indian manner, with feathers and other things, in a level place, the soldiers of Laudonnière being present; and the force sat down in a circle, the chief being in the middle. A fire was then lighted on his left, and two great vessels full of water were set on his right. Then the chief, after rolling his eyes as if excited by anger, uttering some sounds deep down in his throat, and making various gestures, all at once raised a horrid yell; and all his soldiers repeated this yell, striking their hips, and rattling their weapons. Then the chief, taking a wooden platter of water, turned toward the sun, and worshipped it; praying to it for a victory over the enemy, and that, as he should now scatter the water that he had dipped up in the wooden platter, so might their blood be poured out. Then he flung the water with a great cast up into the air; and, as it fell down upon his men, he added, "As I have done with this water, so I pray that you may do with the blood of your enemies." Then he poured the water in the other vase upon the fire, and said, "So may you be able to extinguish your enemies, and bring back their scalps." Then they all arose, and set off by land up the river, upon their expedition.

Laudonnière, having received some of the men of the chief, Holata Utina, or Outina, living about forty miles south from the French fort, and who had been taken in a previous expedition by his enemy Saturioua, sent them back to their chief, upon which a solemn league was made, and mutual friendship promised. This treaty was made for the reason that the only road, whether by land or by the rivers, to the Apalatcy Mountains, in which gold, silver, and brass [aes] are found, was through the dominions of this chief; and it was in his friendship, now of scarcely a year's standing, that the French trusted to obtain free access to those mountains. As this friendship, however, was as yet existing, he asked Laudonnière for some arquebusiers, as he wished to make war on an enemy; on which twenty-five were sent him, under D'Ottigny, Laudonnière's lieutenant. The chief received them with great delight, as he made sure of the victory through their assistance; for the fame of the arquebuses had penetrated throughout all that region, and had struck all with terror. The chief having therefore completed his preparations, the army marched. Their first day's journey was easy; the second very difficult, being through swamps thickly overgrown with thorns and brambles. Here the Indians were obliged to carry the French on their shoulders, which was the greater relief by reason of the extreme heats. At length they reached the enemy's territories, when the chief halted his force, and summoning an aged sorcerer, more than a hundred and twenty years old, directed him to report what was the state of affairs with the enemy. The sorcerer accordingly made ready a place in the middle of the army, and, seeing the shield which D'Ottigny's page was carrying, asked to take it. On receiving it, he laid it on the ground, and drew around it a circle, upon which he inscribed various characters and signs. Then he knelt down on the shield, and sat on his heels, so that no part of him touched the earth, and began to recite some unknown words in a low tone, and to make various gestures, as if engaged in a vehement discourse. This lasted for a quarter of an hour, when he began to assume an appearance so frightful that he was hardly like a human being; for he twisted his limbs so that the bones could be heard to snap out of place, and did many other unnatural things.

R. Holata Outina.

OUTINA, WITH THE HELP OF THE FRENCH, GAINS A VICTORY OVER HIS ENEMY POTANOU

This report so terrified the chief that he began to consider not how to come up with the enemy, but how to get safe back again. But D'Ottigny, greatly vexed at the idea of making such exertions only to return without bringing any thing to pass, threatened to consider him a base chief, and of no courage, if he should not risk an action; and, by force of reproaches and some threats too, brought him to order an attack. He, however, put the French in the advance, as they were quite willing to have him do; and indeed, unless they had sustained the whole brunt of the battle, killing very many of the enemy, and putting to flight the army of the chief Potanou, there is no question but Outina would have been routed; for it became evident that the sorcerer had made a true report of the facts, and he must certainly have been possessed by a devil. Outina, however, quite contented with the flight of the enemy, recalled his men, and marched for home, to the great wrath of D'Ottigny, who wished to follow up the victory.

R.Holata Outina.

Order of march observed by Outina
on a military expedition

When Saturioua went to war, his men preserved no order, but went along one after another, just as it happened. On the contrary, his enemy Holata Outina, whose name, as I now remember, means "king of many kings," and who was much more powerful than he as regards both wealth, and number of his subjects, used to march with regular ranks, like an organized army; himself marching alone in the middle of the whole force, painted red. On the wings, or horns, of his order of march were his young men, the swiftest of whom, also painted red, acted as advanced guards and scouts for reconnoitring the enemy. These are able to follow up the traces of the enemy by scent, as dogs do wild beasts; and, when they come upon such traces, they immediately return to the army to report. And, as we make use of trumpets and drums in our armies to promulgate orders, so they have heralds, who by cries of certain sorts direct when to halt, or to advance, or to attack, or to perform any other military duty. After sunset they halt, and are never wont to give battle. For encamping, they are arranged in squads of ten each, the bravest men being put in squads by themselves. When the chief has chosen the place of encampment for the night, in open fields or woods, and after he has eaten, and is established by himself, the quartermasters place ten of these squads of the bravest men in a circle around him. About ten paces outside of this circle is placed another line of twenty squads; at twenty yards farther, another of forty squads; and so on, increasing the number and distance of these lines, according to the size of the army.

R. Holata Outina.

How Outina's men treated the slain of the enemy

At no time while the French were acting along with the great chief Holata Outina in his wars against his enemies, was there any combat which could be called a regular battle; but all their military operations consisted either in secret incursions, or in skirmishes as light troops, fresh men being constantly sent out in place of any who retired. Whichever side first slew an enemy, no matter how insignificant the person, claimed the victory, even though losing a greater number of men. In their skirmishes, any who fall are instantly dragged off by persons detailed for the purpose; who, with slips of reeds sharper than any steel blade, cut the skin of the head to the bone, from front to back, all the way around, and pull it off with the hair, more than a foot and a half long, still adhering, done up in a knot on the crown, and with that lower down around the forehead and back cut short into a ring about two fingers wide, like the rim of a hat. Then, if they have time, they dig a hole in the ground, and make a fire, kindling it with some which they keep burning in moss, done up in skins, and carry round with them at their belts; and then dry these scalps to a state as hard as parchment. They also are accustomed, after a battle, to cut off with these reed knives the arms of the dead near the shoulders, and their legs near the hips, breaking the bones, when laid bare, with a club, and then to lay these fresh broken, and still running with blood, over the same fires to be dried. Then hanging them, and the scalps also, to the ends of their spears, they carry them off home in triumph. I used to be astonished at one habit of theirs,—for I was one of the party whom Laudonnière sent out under M. d'Ottigny,—which was, that they never left the field of battle without shooting an arrow as deep as they could into the arms of each of the corpses of the enemy, after mutilating them as above; an operation which was sometimes sufficiently dangerous, unless those engaged in it had an escort of soldiers.

Trophies and ceremonies after a victory

After returning from a military expedition, they assemble in a place set apart for the purpose, to which they bring the legs, arms, and scalps which they have taken from the enemy, and with solemn formalities fix them up on tall poles set in the ground in a row. Then they all, men and women, sit down on the ground in a circle before these members; while the sorcerer, holding a small image in his hand, goes through a form of cursing the enemy, uttering in a low voice, according to their manner, a thousand imprecations. At the side of the circle opposite to him, there are placed three men kneeling down, one of whom holds in both hands a club, with which he pounds on a flat stone, marking time to every word of the sorcerer. At each side of him, the other two hold in each hand the fruit of a certain plant, something like a gourd or pumpkin, which has been dried, opened at each end, its marrow and seeds taken out, and then mounted on a stick, and charged with small stones or seeds of some kind. These they rattle after the fashion of a bell, accompanying the words of the sorcerer with a sort of song after their manner. They have such a celebration as this every time they take any of the enemy.

R Holata Oulina.

35

Hermaphrodites, partaking of the nature of each sex, are quite common in these parts, and are considered odious by the Indians themselves, who, however, employ them, as they are strong, instead of beasts of burden. When a chief goes out to war, the hermaphrodites carry the provisions. When any Indian is dead of wounds or disease, two hermaphrodites take a couple of stout poles, fasten cross-pieces on them, and attach to these a mat woven of reeds. On this they place the deceased, with a skin under his head, a second bound around his body, a third around one thigh, a fourth around one leg. Why these are so used, I did not ascertain; but I imagine by way of ornament, as in some cases they do not go so far, but put the skin upon one leg only. Then they take thongs of hide, three or four fingers broad, fasten the ends to the ends of the poles, and put the middle over their heads, which are remarkably hard; and in this manner they carry the deceased to the place of burial. Persons having contagious diseases are also carried to places appointed for the purpose, on the shoulders of the hermaphrodites, who supply them with food, and take care of them, until they get quite well again.

THE CHIEF APPLIED TO BY WOMEN WHOSE
HUSBANDS HAVE DIED IN WAR OR BY DISEASE

The wives of such as have fallen in war, or died by disease, are accustomed to get together on some day which they find convenient for approaching the chief. They come before him with great weeping and outcry, sit down on their heels, hide their faces in their hands, and with much clamor and lamentation require of the chief vengeance for their dead husbands, the means of living during their widowhood, and permission to marry again at the end of the time appointed by law. The chief, sympathizing with them, assents; and they go home weeping and lamenting, so as to show the strength of their love for the deceased. After some days spent in this mourning, they proceed to the graves of their husbands, carrying the weapons and drinking-cups of the dead, and there they mourn for them again, and perform other feminine ceremonies.

Ceremonies of women mourning for their deceased husbands

After coming to the graves of their husbands, they cut off their hair below the ears, and scatter it upon the graves; and then cast upon them the weapons and drinking-shells of the deceased, as memorials of brave men. This done, they return home, but are not allowed to marry again until their hair has grown long enough to cover their shoulders. They let their nails grow long both on fingers and toes, cutting the former away, however, at the sides, so as to leave them very sharp, the men especially; and, when they take one of the enemy, they sink their nails deep in his forehead, and tear down the skin, so as to wound and blind him.

Their way of curing diseases is as follows: They put up a bench or platform of sufficient length and breadth for the patient, as seen in the plate, and lay the sick person upon it with his face up or down, according to the nature of his complaint; and, cutting into the skin of the forehead with a sharp shell, they suck out blood with their mouths, and spit it into an earthen vessel or a gourd bottle. Women who are suckling boys, or who are with child, come and drink this blood, particularly if it is that of a strong young man; as it is expected to make their milk better, and to render the children who have the benefit of it bolder and more energetic. For those who are laid on their faces, they prepare fumigations by throwing certain seeds on hot coals; the smoke being made to pass through the nose and mouth into all parts of the body, and thus to act as a vomit, or to overcome and expel the cause of the disease. They have a certain plant whose name has escaped me, which the Brazilians call *petum,* and the Spaniards *tapaco.* The leaves of this, carefully dried, they place in the wider part of a pipe; and setting them on fire, and putting the other end in their mouths, they inhale the smoke so strongly, that it comes out at their mouths and noses, and operates powerfully to expel the humors. In particular, they are extremely subject to the venereal disease, for curing which they have remedies of their own, supplied by nature.

43

The Indians cultivate the earth diligently; and the men know how to make a kind of hoe from fishes' bones, which they fit to wooden handles, and with these they prepare the land well enough, as the soil is light. When the ground is sufficiently broken up and levelled, the women come with beans and millet, or maize. Some go first with a stick, and make holes, in which the others place the beans, or grains of maize. After planting they leave the fields alone, as the winter in that country, situated between the west and the north, is pretty cold for about three months, being from the 24th of December to the 15th of March; and during that time, as they go naked, they shelter themselves in the woods. When the winter is over, they return to their homes to wait for their crops to ripen. After gathering in their harvest, they store the whole of it for the year's use, not employing any part of it in trade, unless, perhaps, some barter is made for some little household article.

Industry of the Floridians in depositing
their crops in the public granary

There are in that region a great many islands, producing abundance of various kinds of fruits, which they gather twice a year, and carry home in canoes, and store up in roomy low granaries built of stones and earth, and roofed thickly with palm-branches and a kind of soft earth fit for the purpose. These granaries are usually erected near some mountain, or on the bank of some river, so as to be out of the sun's rays, in order that the contents may keep better. Here they also store up any other provisions which they may wish to preserve, and the remainder of their stores; and they go and get them as need may require, without any apprehensions of being defrauded. Indeed, it is to be wished, that, among the Christians, avarice prevailed no more than among them, and tormented no more the minds of men.

Bringing in wild animals, fish, and other stores

At a set time every year they gather in all sorts of wild animals, fish, and even crocodiles; these are then put in baskets, and loaded upon a sufficient number of the curly-haired hermaphrodites above mentioned, who carry them on their shoulders to the storehouse. This supply, however, they do not resort to unless in case of the last necessity. In such event, in order to preclude any dissension, full notice is given to all interested; for they live in the utmost harmony among themselves. The chief, however, is at liberty to take whatever of this supply he may choose.

Mode of drying fish, wild animals, and other provisions

In order to keep these animals longer, they are in the habit of preparing them as follows: They set up in the earth four stout forked stakes; and on these they lay others, so as to form a sort of grating. On this they lay their game, and then build a fire underneath, so as to harden them in the smoke. In this process they use a great deal of care to have the drying perfectly performed, to prevent the meat from spoiling, as the picture shows. I suppose this stock to be laid in for their winter's supply in the woods, as at that time we could never obtain the least provision from them. For the like reason their granaries, as was related, are placed close under some rock or cliff, near a river, and not far from some deep forest, so that when necessary they can carry a supply in canoes.

The Indians have a way of hunting deer which we never saw before. They manage to put on the skins of the largest which have before been taken, in such a manner, with the heads on their own heads, so that they can see out through the eyes as through a mask. Thus accoutred, they can approach close to the deer without frightening them. They take advantage of the time when the animals come to drink at the river, and, having their bow and arrows all ready, easily shoot them, as they are very plentiful in those regions. It is usual, however, to protect the left arm with the bark of the branch of a tree, to keep it from being grazed by the bow-string,— a practice which they have learned naturally enough. They know how to prepare deer-skins, not with iron instruments, but with shells, in a surprisingly excellent manner; indeed, I do not believe that any European could do it as well.

KILLING CROCODILES *

Their way of attacking crocodiles is as follows: They put up, near a river, a little hut full of cracks and holes, and in this they station a watchman, so that he can see the crocodiles, and hear them, a good way off; for, when driven by hunger, they come out of the rivers, and crawl about on the islands after prey, and, if they find none, they make such a frightful noise that it can be heard for half a mile. Then the watchman calls the rest of the watch, who are in readiness; and, taking a portion, ten or twelve feet long, of the stem of a tree, they go out to find the monster, who is crawling along with his mouth wide open, all ready to catch one of them if he can; and with the greatest quickness they push the pole, small end first, as deep as possible down his throat, so that the roughness and irregularity of the bark may hold it from being got out again. Then they turn the crocodile over on his back, and with clubs and arrows pound and pierce his belly, which is softer; for his back, especially if he is an old one, is impenetrable, being protected by hard scales. This is their way of hunting crocodiles; by which they are, nevertheless, so much annoyed that they have to keep up a regular watch against them both day and night, as we should do against the most dangerous enemy.

* Probably alligators

FLORIDIANS CROSSING OVER TO AN ISLAND
TO TAKE THEIR PLEASURE

That country abounds in most delightful islands, as the first pictures of our series show. The rivers are not deep; but the water, which comes not higher than to the breast, is very clear and pure. When they desire to make a little pleasure excursion with their wives and children, to one of these islands, they cross over by swimming, in which they are very skilful; or, if they have young children, by wading. The mother can carry three children at a time, the smallest on one shoulder, and holding it by one arm, the other two holding on to her under her arms; while in her other hand she holds up a basket full of fruit or other provisions for the occasion. When there is any fear of the enemy, the men take their bows and arrows; and, to keep them from being wet, they attach the quiver to the hair of the head, and hold up in one hand a bow already strung, and an arrow, for instant defence if necessary: as in the picture.

57

At the time of year when they are in the habit of feasting each other, they employ cooks, who are chosen on purpose for the business. These, first of all, take a great round earthen vessel (which they know how to make and to burn so that water can be boiled in it as well as in our kettles), and place it over a large wood-fire, which one of them drives with a fan very effectively, holding it in the hand. The head cook now puts the things to be cooked into the great pot; others put water for washing into a hole in the ground; another brings water in a utensil that serves for a bucket; another pounds on a stone the aromatics that are to be used for seasoning; while the women are picking over or preparing the viands. Although they have great festivities, after their manner, yet they are very temperate in eating, and, in consequence, they live to a great age; for one of their inferior chiefs affirmed to me that he was three hundred years old, and that his father, whom he pointed out to me, was fifty years older; indeed, this last personage, I confess, looked like nothing but the bones of a man covered with a skin. Such facts might well make us Christians ashamed, who are so immoderate in indulgence both in eating and drinking, who shorten our own lives thereby, and who richly deserve to be put under the authority of these savages and of brute beasts, to be taught sobriety.

Proceedings of the Floridians
in deliberating on important affairs

The chief and his nobles are accustomed during certain days of the year to meet early every morning for this express purpose in a public place, in which a long bench is constructed, having at the middle of it a projecting part laid with nine round trunks of trees, for the chief's seat. On this he sits by himself, for distinction's sake; and here the rest come to salute him, one at a time, the oldest first, by lifting both hands twice to the height of the head, and saying, "Ha, he, ya, ha, ha." To this the rest answer, "Ha, ha." Each, as he completes his salutation, takes his seat on the bench. If any question of importance is to be discussed, the chief calls upon his *laüas* (that is, his priests) and upon the elders, one at a time, to deliver their opinions. They decide upon nothing until they have held a number of councils over it, and they deliberate very sagely before deciding. Meanwhile the chief orders the women to boil some *casina;* which is a drink prepared from the leaves of a certain root, and which they afterwards pass through a strainer. The chief and his councillors being now seated in their places, one stands before him, and, spreading forth his hands wide open, asks a blessing upon the chief and the others who are to drink. Then the cupbearer brings the hot drink in a capacious shell, first to the chief, and then, as the chief directs, to the rest in their order, in the same shell. They esteem this drink so highly, that no one is allowed to drink it in council unless he has proved himself a brave warrior. Moreover, this drink has the quality of at once throwing into a sweat whoever drinks it. On this account those who cannot keep it down, but whose stomachs reject it, are not intrusted with any difficult commission, or any military responsibility, being considered unfit, for they often have to go three or four days without food; but one who can drink this liquor can go for twenty-four hours afterwards without eating or drinking. In military expeditions, also, the only supplies which the hermaphrodites carry consist of gourd bottles or wooden vessels full of this drink. It strengthens and nourishes the body, and yet does not fly to the head; as we have observed on occasion of these feasts of theirs.

61

Construction of fortified towns among the Floridians

The Indians are accustomed to build their fortified towns as follows: A position is selected near the channel of some swift stream. They level it as even as possible, and then dig a ditch in a circle around the site, in which they set thick round pales, close together, to twice the height of a man; and they carry this paling some ways past the beginning of it, spiral-wise, to make a narrow entrance admitting not more than two persons abreast. The course of the stream is also diverted to this entrance; and at each end of it they are accustomed to erect a small round building, each full of cracks and holes, and built, considering their means, with much elegance. In these they station as sentinels men who can smell the traces of an enemy at a great distance, and who, as soon as they perceive such traces, set off to discover them. As soon as they find them, they set up a cry which summons those within the town to the defence, armed with bows and arrows and clubs. The chief's dwelling stands in the middle of the town, and is partly underground, in consequence of the sun's heat. Around this are the houses of the principal men, all lightly roofed with palm-branches, as they are occupied only nine months in the year; the other three, as has been related, being spent in the woods. When they come back, they occupy their houses again; and, if they find that the enemy has burnt them down, they build others of similar materials. Thus magnificent are the palaces of the Indians.

How they set on fire an enemy's town

For the enemy, eager for revenge, sometimes will creep up by night in the utmost silence, and reconnoitre to see if the watch be asleep. If they find everything silent, they approach the rear of the town, set fire to some dry moss from trees, which they prepare in a particular manner, and fasten to the heads of their arrows. They then fire these into the town, so as to ignite the roofs of the houses, which are made of palm-branches thoroughly dried with the summer heats. As soon as they see that the roofs are burning, they make off as fast as possible, before they are discovered, and they move so swiftly that it is a hard matter to overtake them; and meanwhile also the fire is giving the people in the town enough to do to save themselves from it, and get it under. Such are the stratagems used in war by the Indians for firing the enemy's towns; but the damage done is trifling, as it amounts only to the labor required for putting up new houses.

How sentinels are punished for sleeping on their posts

But, when the burning of the town has happened in consequence of the negligence of the watch, the penalty is as follows: The chief takes his place alone on his bench, those next to him in authority being seated on another long bench curved in a half circle; and the executioner orders the culprit to kneel down before the chief. He then sets his left foot on the delinquent's back; and, taking in both hands a club of ebony or some other hard wood, worked to an edge at the sides, he strikes him on the head with it, so severely as almost to split the skull open. The same penalty is inflicted for some other crime reckoned capital among them; for we saw two persons punished in this same way.

How they declare war

A chief who declares war against his enemy does not send a herald to do it, but orders some arrows, having locks of hair fastened at the notches, to be stuck up along the public ways; as we observed when, after taking the chief Outina prisoner, we carried him around to the towns under his authority, to make them furnish us provisions.

First-born children sacrificed to the chief with solemn ceremonies

Their custom is to offer up the first-born son to the chief. When the day for the sacrifice is notified to the chief, he proceeds to a place set apart for the purpose, where there is a bench for him, on which he takes his seat. In the middle of the area before him is a wooden stump two feet high, and as many thick, before which the mother sits on her heels, with her face covered in her hands, lamenting the loss of her child. The principal one of her female relatives or friends now offers the child to the chief in worship, after which the women who have accompanied the mother form a circle, and dance around with demonstrations of joy, but without joining hands. She who holds the child goes and dances in the middle, singing some praises of the chief. Meanwhile, six Indians, chosen for the purpose, take their stand apart in a certain place in the open area; and midway among them the sacrificing officer, who is decorated with a sort of magnificence, and holds a club. The ceremonies being through, the sacrificer takes the child, and slays it in honor of the chief, before them all, upon the wooden stump. This offering was on one occasion performed in our presence.

SOLEMNITIES AT CONSECRATING THE SKIN OF
A STAG TO THE SUN

The subjects of the chief Outina were accustomed every year, a little before their spring, that is, in the end of February, to take the skin of the largest stag they could get, keeping the horns on it; to stuff it full of all the choicest sorts of roots that grow among them, and to hang long wreaths or garlands of the best fruits on the horns, neck, and other parts of the body. Thus decorated, they carried it, with music and songs, to a very large and splendid level space, where they set it up on a very high tree, with the head and breast toward the sunrise. They then offered prayers to the sun, that he would cause to grow on their lands good things such as those offered him. The chief, with his sorcerer, stands nearest the tree, and offers the prayer; the common people, placed at a distance, make responses. Then the chief and all the rest, saluting the sun, depart, leaving the deer's hide there until the next year. This ceremony they repeat annually.

THE YOUTH AT THEIR EXERCISES

Their youth are trained in running, and a prize is offered for him who can run longest without stopping; and they frequently practise with the bow. They also play a game of ball, as follows: in the middle of an open space is set up a tree some eight or nine fathoms high, with a square frame woven of twigs on the top; this is to be hit with the ball, and he who strikes it first gets a prize. They are also fond of amusing themselves with hunting and fishing.

THE DISPLAY WITH WHICH A QUEEN ELECT
IS BROUGHT TO THE KING

When a king chooses to take a wife, he directs the tallest and handsomest of the daughters of the chief men to be selected. Then a seat is made on two stout poles, and covered with the skin of some rare sort of animal, while it is set off with a structure of boughs, bending over forward so as to shade the head of the sitter. The queen elect having been placed on this, four strong men take up the poles, and support them on their shoulders; each carrying in one hand a forked wooden stick to support the pole at halting. Two more walk at the sides; each carrying on a staff a round screen elegantly made, to protect the queen from the sun's rays. Others go before, blowing upon trumpets made of bark, which are smaller above, and larger at the farther end, and having only the two orifices, one at each end. They are hung with small oval balls of gold, silver, and brass, for the sake of a finer combination of sounds. Behind follow the most beautiful girls that can be found, elegantly decorated with necklaces and armlets of pearls, each carrying in her hand a basket full of choice fruits; and belted below the navel, and down to the thighs, with the moss of certain trees, to cover their nakedness. After them come the body-guards.

Solemnities at the Reception
of the Queen by the King

With this display the queen is brought to the king in a place arranged for the purpose, where a good-sized platform is built up of round logs, having on either side a long bench where the chief men are seated. The king sits on the platform on the right-hand side. The queen, who is placed on the left, is congratulated by him on her accession, and told why he chose her for his first wife. She, with a certain modest majesty, and holding her fan in her hand, answers with as good a grace as she can. Then the young women form a circle without joining hands, and with a costume differing from the usual one; for their hair is tied at the back of the neck, and then left to flow over the shoulders and back; and they wear a broad girdle below the navel, having in front something like a purse, which hangs down so as to cover their nudity. To the rest of this girdle are hung ovals of gold and silver, coming down upon the thighs, so as to tinkle when they dance, while at the same time they chant the praises of the king and queen. In this dance they all raise and lower their hands together. All the men and women have the ends of their ears pierced, and pass through them small oblong fish-bladders, which when inflated shine like pearls, and which, being dyed red, look like a light-colored carbuncle. It is wonderful that men so savage should be capable of such tasteful inventions.

THE KING AND QUEEN TAKING A WALK
FOR THEIR AMUSEMENT

Sometimes the king likes to take a walk in the evening in a neighboring wood, alone with his principal wife, wearing a deer's hide so elegantly prepared, and painted of various colors, so that nothing more beautifully finished can be seen anywhere. Two young men walk at his sides, carrying fans to make a breeze for him; while a third, ornamented with little gold and silver balls hanging to his belt, goes behind, and holds up the deer's hide, so that it shall not drag on the ground. The queen and her handmaids are adorned with belts hung on the shoulders or around the body, made of a kind of moss that grows on some trees; with slender filaments which are attached to each other, after the fashion of links of a chain, of a bluish-green color, and so beautiful in texture that it might be mistaken for filaments of silk. The trees laden with this moss are beautiful to see; for it sometimes hangs down from the highest boughs of a very tall tree to the ground. While hunting once with some of my fellow-soldiers in the woods near King Saturioua's residence, I saw him and his queen thus decorated.

The reader should be informed that all these chiefs and their wives ornament their skin with punctures arranged so as to make certain designs, as the following pictures show. Doing this sometimes makes them sick for seven or eight days. They rub the punctured places with a certain herb, which leaves an indelible color. For the sake of further ornament and magnificence, they let the nails of their fingers and toes grow, scraping them down at the sides with a certain shell, so that they are left very sharp. They are also in the habit of painting the skin around their mouths of a blue color.

When a chief in that province dies, he is buried with great solemnities; his drinking-cup is placed on the grave, and many arrows are planted in the earth about the mound itself. His subjects mourn for him three whole days and nights, without taking any food. All the other chiefs, his friends, mourn in like manner; and both men and women, in testimony of their love for him, cut off more than half their hair. Besides this, for six months afterwards certain chosen women three times every day, at dawn, noon, and twilight, mourn for the deceased king with a great howling. And all his household stuff is put into his house, which is set on fire, and the whole burned up together.

In like manner, when their priests die, they are buried in their own houses; which are then set on fire, and burned up with all their furniture.

Mode of collecting gold in streams running from the Apalatcy Mountains

A great way from the place where our fort was built, are great mountains, called in the Indian language Apalatcy; in which, as the map shows, arise three great rivers, in the sands of which are found much gold, silver, and brass, mixed together. Accordingly, the natives dig ditches in these streams, into which the sand brought down by the current falls by gravity. Then they collect it out, and carry it away to a place by itself, and after a time collect again what continues to fall in. They then convey it in canoes down the great river which we named the River of May, and which empties into the sea. The Spaniards have been able to use for their advantage the wealth thus obtained.

MURDER OF PIERRE GAMBRÉ, A FRENCHMAN

I have spoken in my Brief Account of one Pierre Gambré, a Frenchman, who obtained a license from Laudonnière for carrying goods, and trading, throughout the province; and who was successful enough not only to accumulate considerable means, but also to marry into the family of a certain chief of the country. Being seized with an earnest desire of returning to see his friends at the fort, he urged his new relative until he got permission to go, but on condition of returning within a fixed number of months; and a canoe was provided for him besides, and two Indians to convey him. The goods which he had obtained were stowed in the boat; and his Indian companions murdered him while on the journey, while he was stooping over to make a fire. This was done partly in revenge, as he had, while acting in the chief's absence in his stead, beaten one of them with his fists; and partly out of greediness for the riches which the soldier had with him in the boat. These they took, and fled; and the facts were unknown for a long time.

This picture, not to interrupt the series of those preceding it, is put last; nor would it have been inserted at all, had not the author of the Brief Account remembered the circumstances.

The Narrative of Le Moyne

THE FIRST ACCOUNT in this *Settlement of Florida* was written by the French artist Jacques le Moyne de Morgues and published in Latin by the Flemish engraver and editor, Théodor de Bry in *Brevis Narratio* (Frankfort, 1591). In addition to the historical narrative, a map of Florida and forty-two illustrations by Le Moyne were engraved and printed by De Bry. The drawings of Le Moyne depict the various activities of Florida Indians in an imaginative and romantic manner and the artist also gives brief explanations of the pictures. The Florida writings of Le Moyne were translated into English by Fred B. Perkins and published as the *Narrative of Le Moyne* (Boston, 1875).

The Narrative of Le Moyne

harles IX., King of France, having been notified by the Admiral de Châtillon that there was too much delay in sending forward the re-enforcements needed by the small body of French whom Jean Ribaud had left to maintain the French dominion in Florida, gave orders to the admiral to fit out such a fleet as was required for the purpose. The admiral, in the meanwhile, recommended to the king a nobleman of the name of Renaud de Laudonnière; a person well known at court, and of varied abilities, though experienced not so much in military as in naval affairs. The king accordingly appointed him his own lieutenant, and appropriated for the expedition the sum of a hundred thousand francs. The admiral, who was a man endowed with all the virtues, and eminent for Christian piety, was so zealous for the faithful doing of the king's business, as to give special instructions to Laudonnière, exhorting him in particular to use all manner of diligence in doing his duty, and first of all, since he professed to be a religious man, to select the right sort of men, and such as feared God, to be of his company. He would do well, in the next place, to engage as many skilled mechanics of all kinds as possible. In order to give him better facilities for these purposes he received a royal commission, bearing the king's seal.

Laudonnière, accordingly repaired to Havre-de-Grâce, where he proceeded to get his ships ready, and, according to his orders, with the greatest diligence sought out good men all over the kingdom; so that I can safely assert that men of remarkable skill in all sorts of mechanical employments resorted to him. There also assembled a number of noble youths of ancient families, drawn only by the desire of viewing foreign countries; for they asked no pay, volunteering for the expedition at their own cost and charges. The soldiers were chosen veterans, every man competent to act as an officer in time of battle. From Dieppe were obtained the two best navigators of our times, Michael le Vasseur and his brother Thomas le Vasseur, both of whom were employed in the king's naval service. I also received orders to join the expedition, and to report to M. de Laudonnière.

All who came he received with courtesy and with magnificent promises. As, however, I was not unaware that the gentlemen of the court are in the habit of being liberal with their promises, I asked for some positive statements of his own views, and of the particular object which the king desired to obtain in commanding my services. Upon this he promised that no services except honorable ones should be required of me; and he informed me that my special duty, when we should reach the Indies, would be to map the seacoast, and lay down the position of towns, the depth and course of rivers, and the harbors; and to represent also the dwellings of the natives, and whatever in the province might seem worthy of observation: all of which I performed to the best of my ability, as I showed his majesty, when, after having escaped from the remarkable perfidies and atrocious cruelties of the Spaniards, I returned to France.

On the 20th April, 1564, our three ships set sail from Hâvre-de-Grace, and steered direct for the Fortunate Islands, or, as seafaring men call them, the Canaries. Sailing thence, on the tropic we made the Antilles Islands, at one of which, called Dominica, we watered, losing, however, two men. Making sail again, we reached the coast of Florida, or New France as it is called, on Thursday, 22d June.

M. de Laudonnière having reconnoitred the stream named by Ribaud the River of May, and finding it of easy navigation for ships, and offering a suitable place for a fort, set promptly about preparing to erect one, and sent back to France his largest ship, the "Elizabeth of Honfleur," commanded by Jean Lucas. Meanwhile, all the seashore was occupied by immense numbers of men and women, who kept up fires, and against whom we naturally thought it necessary to be much on our guard. Gradually, however, it appeared that to injure us was the last thing in their thoughts: on the other hand, they showed numerous testimonies of friendship and liking, being seized with great admiration at finding our flesh so different from theirs in softness and tenderness, and our garments so different from their own. The commodities which we received from these new dealers were in great part such things as they value most, being for the support of life or the protection of the body. Such were grains of maize roasted, or ground into flour, or whole ears of it; smoked lizards or other wild animals, such as they consider great delicacies; and various kinds of roots, some for food, and some for medicine. When they found out after a time that the French were more desirous of metals and minerals, some brought them. M. de Laudonnière, who soon perceived that our men were acting avariciously in their dealing, now forbade, on pain of death, any trading or exchange with the Indians for gold, silver, or minerals, unless all such should be put into a common stock for the benefit of all.

In the meantime several chiefs visited our commander, and signified to him that they were under the authority of a certain king named Saturioua, within the limits of whose dominions we were, whose dwelling was near us, and who could muster a force of some thousands of men. This information was thought good reason for hastening the completion of our fort. King Saturioua himself, on his part, like a prudent commander, sent out his scouts from day to day, to see what we were about; and being advised by them that we had marked out a triangle by stretching cords, and were digging up the earth on the lines of it, he became desirous of seeing for himself. He sent forward, however, some two hours in advance of his own appearance, an officer with a company of a hundred and twenty able-bodied men, armed with bows, arrows, clubs, and darts, and adorned, after the Indian manner, with their riches; such as feathers of different kinds, necklaces of a select sort of shells, bracelets of fishes' teeth, girdles of silver-colored balls, some round and some oblong; and having many pearls fastened on their legs. Many of them had also hanging to their legs round flat plates of gold, silver, or brass, so that in walking they tinkled like little bells. This officer, having made his announcement, proceeded to cause shelter to be erected on a small height nearby, of branches of palms, laurels, mastics, and other odoriferous trees, for the accom-modation of the king. From this point the king could see whatever was going on within our lines, and a few tents and military supplies and baggage, which we had not yet found time to get under cover; as our first business was to get our fort com-pleted, rather than to put up huts, which could be easily erected more at leisure afterwards.

M. de Laudonnière, upon receiving the message of the officer, so disposed his force as to be prepared for a stout resistance in case of attack, although they had no ammunition on shore for their defence. In the next place, as he had himself while with Ribaud on a former occasion stopped here, and seen this same chief, had learned a few words of his language, and knew the ceremonial with which he expected to be received; and as one of his men, an intelligent and active person, who had also been here with Ribaud, and was now a captain, possessed the same information,--M. de Laudonnière decided that it would be best for none to approach the king's presence except himself, M. d'Ottigny his second in command, and Capt. La Caille just referred to.

The king was accompanied by seven or eight hundred men, handsome, strong, well-made, and active fellows, the best-trained and swiftest of his force, all under arms as if on a mili-tary expedition. Before him marched fifty youths with javelins or spears; and behind these, and next to himself, were twenty pipers, who produced a wild noise, without musical harmony or regularity, but only blowing away with all their might, each trying to be the loudest. Their instruments were nothing but a thick sort of reeds, or canes, with two openings; one at the top to blow into, and the other at the other end for the wind to come out of, like organ-pipes or whistles. On his right hand limped his soothsayer, and on the left was his chief counsellor; without which two personages he never proceeded on any matter whatever. He entered the place prepared for him alone, and sat down in it after the Indian manner; that is, by squatting on the ground like an ape or any other animal. Then having looked all around, and having observed our little force drawn up in line of battle, he ordered MM. de Laudonnière and d'Ottigny to be invited into his tabernacle, where he delivered to them a long oration, which they understood only in part. He did, however, inquire who we were, why we had landed on his territory rather than elsewhere, and what was our purpose. M. de Laudonnière replied by the mouth of Capt. La Caille, who, as was mentioned, had some knowledge of the language, that he was sent by a most powerful king, called the King of France, to offer a treaty by which he should become a friend to the king here, and to his allies, and an enemy to their enemies; an announce- ment which the chief received with much pleasure. Gifts were then exchanged in pledge of perpetual friendship and alliance. This done, the king approached nearer to our force, and greatly admired our arms, particularly the arquebuses. Upon coming up to the ditch of our fort, he took measurements both within and without; and perceiving that the earth was being taken from the ditch, and laid into a rampart, he asked what was the use of the operation. He was told in reply that we were going to put up a building that would hold all of us, and that many small houses were to be erected inside of it; at which he expressed admiration, and a desire to see it completed as soon as possible. To this end, he was therefore asked to give us the help of some of his followers in the work. He consented, and sent us eighty of his stoutest men, most used to labor, who were of great assistance to us, and much hastened the completion both of our fort and cabins. Having given his orders about this, he himself went away.

While all this was going on, every man of our force-- noblemen, soldiers, artificers, sailors, and all--was hard at work to get our post in a state of defence against an enemy, and to get up a shelter from the weather; and every man was making sure, from the amount of the gifts and trading so far, that he would quickly become rich.

The fort being now completed, and a residence for himself,

as well as a large building to contain the provisions and other indispensable military supplies, M. de Laudonnière proceeded to shorten the allowance of food and drink: so that, after three weeks, only one glass of spirit and water, half and half, was given out daily per man; and as for provisions, which it had been hoped would be abundant in this New World, none at all were found; and, unless the natives had furnished us from their own stores from day to day, some of us must assuredly have perished from starvation, especially such as did not know how to use fire-arms in hunting.

In the meanwhile M. de Laudonnière ordered his chief artificer, Jean des Hayes of Dieppe, to build two shallops, to be, according to my recollection, of thirty-five or forty feet keel, for exploring in the upper waters of the river, and along the seacoast; which were in good season nearly completed.

But by this time the noblemen who had come from France to the New World from ambitious motives only, and with splendid outfits, began to be greatly dissatisfied at finding that they realized none of the advantages which they had imagined, and promised themselves; and complaints began daily to be made by many of them. On the other part M. de Laudonnière himself, who was a man too easily influenced by others, evidently fell into the hands of three or four parasites, and treated with contempt the soldiers, who were just those whom he should have most considered. And, what is far worse, indignation began to be felt by many who professed the desire of living according to the doctrine of the reformed gospel, for the reason that they found themselves without a minister of God's word.

But to return to King Saturioua. This chief sent messengers to M. de Laudonnière, not only to confirm the league which had been made, but also to procure the performance of its conditions, namely, that the latter was to be the friend of the king's friends, and the enemy of his enemies; as he was now organizing an expedition against them. M. de Laudonnière gave an ambiguous reply to these ambassadors; for we had learned, in the course of an extended voyage up the main stream of the River of May, that the enemy of our neighbor King Saturioua was far more powerful than he; and that, moreover, his friendship was indispensable to us for the reason that the road to the Apalatcy Mountains (which we were desirous of reaching, because we were informed that most of the gold and silver which we had received in trade was brought thence) lay through his dominions. Besides, some of our people were already with him, who had already sent to the fort a good deal of gold and silver, and were negotiating with him; for M. de Laudonnière had orders to treat with this great king, Outina, on the same terms as above mentioned.

King Saturioua, having received this cold answer, now came to the fort, which was called Fort Carolina, with some twelve or fifteen hundred men; but finding, to his surprise, that things were greatly changed, that he could no longer get across the ditch, but that there was only one entrance to the post, and that a very narrow one, he came thither, and found Capt. La Caille; who announced to him, that, for the purpose of an interview, he would not be admitted into the fort unless without his men, or at most with not more than twenty of such as he might select. In astonishment at this information, he, however, dissimulated, and entered the fort with twenty of his followers, when everything was exhibited to him. He was terribly frightened himself at the sound of the drums and trumpets, and at the reports of the brass cannon which were fired in his presence; and, when he was told that all his force had run away, he readily believed it, as he would gladly have been farther off himself. This, indeed, made our name great through all those parts; and, in fact, much more than the reality was believed of us. He did, however, after all, notify M. de Laudonnière that his faith was pledged, that his own (King Saturioua's) forces were ready, that his supplies were at hand, and that his own subordinate chiefs were assembled. Failing, however, to obtain what he wished, he set out on his expedition with his own men.

While these affairs were in progress, M. de Laudonnière sent his second ship, commanded by Pierre Capitaine (Petrus Centurio), to France. And now let the reader be pleased to observe how many were those who sought to return home. Among others, one young nobleman, De Marillac by name, was so earnestly desirous of going, that he promised M. de Laudonnière, if the latter would send him back in charge of despatches, to reveal to him matters of the utmost importance touching his life and good name; on condition, however, that the papers containing these revelations should not be opened until after he (Marillac) had embarked. M. de Laudonnière too credulously agreed to this proposition.

On the very day when the ship was to sail, a certain nobleman of the name of M. de Gièvre, of a good family, of the rank of count, one who feared God, and was liked by all, received warning, five or six hours before the time at which the information promised was to be put into the hands of M. de Laudonnière, that he would do well to escape, for that Marillac had laid a plot against him. He accordingly took refuge in the woods to shun the wrath of M. de Laudonniere, to whom Marillac had delivered some infamous libels written, as he asserted, in the hand of M. de Gievre. Their purport was, that Laudonnière had made a wrongful use of the hundred thousand francs given him by the king, since he had brought no supply of provisions over with him; that he had not brought over, as the admiral directed him to do, a minister of God's word; that he bestowed too much of his favor on tattlers and praters, but despised those of real merit; and many other things which I do not now remember.

This exile of M. de Gièvre was unwelcome to many good men, who, however, all kept silence. Gradually, however, some began to be dissatisfied with the bad provision of food, and others with the excess of labor required, and with its severity; particularly certain of the nobles, who considered that they should have been treated with more respect. After various interchange of opinions between individuals, secret consultations began to be held, at first by five or six persons only, but by more and more, until as many as thirty were engaged. But among the first who thus began to consult was one especial favorite of M. de Laudonnière; and it is absolutely certain that it was the very best of the soldiers and noblemen who were engaged in these consultations, and that these influenced the rest; passing over those whom they despised as deficient in shrewdness, and whom, therefore, they did not admit into their counsels.

At a proper time, they addressed themselves to Capt. La Caille, to whom the plan had so far not been revealed, because all knew him to be a man of integrity himself, and who would require the utmost loyalty in all matters of duty from others. Him they now besought, that, as he was the senior captain, he would interest himself in this matter, which concerned all, and that he would consent to deliver to M. de Laudonnière their written statement of their grievances. La Caille promised his assistance; and, as they had selected him to take charge of the matter, he resolved to communicate it to M. de Laudonnière in their name, even though the commander should choose to be displeased, and even though he should risk his own life in consequence; since he believed their petition a proper one. On the next day, which was the Lord's Day, he went early to M. de Laudonnière's house, and requested him, in the name of all the company, to come to the place of public assembly, where he (La Caille) wished to communicate to him a certain matter. All being assembled, M. de Laudonnière appeared with his second in command, M. d'Ottigny; and, silence being proclaimed, Capt. La Caille proceeded to speak as follows--

"Sir, we all, who are here, in the first place protest that we recognize you as the lieutenant of the king, our supreme lord in this province, where our present settlement has been founded in his name; and that we will obey your orders in this very honorable expedition, even though for his majesty's sake our lives shall be poured out before you, as you have already known by experiment in the case of great part of those who are here present, among whom are many of noble rank, who to the neglect of their own advantage have followed you as volunteers at their own expense. In the next place, they would now with all due respect remind you, that, before leaving France, pledges were given to each of them that provisions sufficient for one whole year should be brought over, and that additional supplies should be at hand before those were exhausted; while so far was this from being the case the provisions brought were scarcely one month's supply.

"The Indians, after a time, began to be slow in bringing in supplies, because they found that most of us had no longer anything to give for them; and it is not unknown to you that these savages do not give anything without getting something for it. When after this they found that no commodities at all were forthcoming from any of us, and when the soldiers undertook to extort supplies from them by blows (as some of them began to do, to the great grief of the wiser among them), they deserted the whole neighborhood; so that we lost even those sources of supply which we had, and even with the continued aid of which we had nothing better to expect than the extremity of hunger. In order, therefore, to remedy these difficulties, those present most urgently beseech you to cause the third of the ships which brought us from France, now lying in the river, to be repaired and fitted out; to man her with such persons as you may see fit; and to send her to New Spain, which is not far from this province, to obtain supplies by purchase or otherwise; not doubting that this measure will relieve us. Or, if any better measures shall be suggested, they are ready to acquiesce in them." This was the substance of the address at this assembly.

M. de Laudonnière's reply was brief: that they had no title to require an account from him of his actions; that, as to supplies, he would provide for them, as he still had several casks full of merchandise which he would put into the common stock in order that they might trade with the Indians for provisions; that, as to sending to New Spain, he never would do it; but that instead he would let them take the two shallops that had been begun, for coasting-voyages within two or three hundred miles, by which they would be able to collect provisions enough and to spare. With this reply, the assembly was dismissed.

M. de Laudonnière had been sending out men to explore the remoter parts of the country, more particularly those in the vicinity of the great King Outina, the enemy of our own neighbor, and from whom, by the channel of some of our Frenchmen who had got into relations with him, a good deal of gold and silver had been sent to the fort, as well as pearls, and other valuable articles. But this duty was not allotted to everybody; and, as those employed on it were supposed to be growing rich very fast, many began to be envious of them; and, although M. de Laudonnière promised that everything should be distributed equally to all, many were dissatisfied. For there was one La Roche Ferrière, who being a talkative person, and pretending to know everything, had become so influential with M. de Laudonnière, as to be considered by him almost an oracle. I do not deny that he was a man of ability, and eminently useful in establishing this new acquisition of ours, or that it was due to his continued influence with the King Outina that the commodities referred to were sent into the fort. In return, five or six arquebusiers were sent to him, to be employed in one direction or another, as the occasions or necessities of himself or Outina might require. But, in brief, his operations resulted in Outina's making peace with some enemies of his near the mountains. With reference to this matter, he wrote to M. de Laudonnière to send some one to take his place, as he had various important affairs to communicate touching the king's service, and the honor and advantage of all.

Upon this, M. de Laudonnière at once sent out a person to take the place of La Roche Ferrière; who returned to the fort reporting that he had certain information that all the gold and silver which had been sent to it came from the Apalatcy Mountains, and that the Indians from whom he obtained it knew of no other place to get it, since they had got all they had had so far in warring with three chiefs, named Potanou, Onatheaqua, and Oustaca, who had been preventing the great chief Outina from taking possession of these mountains. Moreover, La Roche Ferrière brought with him a piece of rock mined in those mountains, containing a sufficiently good display of gold and brass. He therefore requested permission of M. de Laudonnière to undertake the long journey by which he hoped he could reach these three chiefs, and examine the state of things about them. Having accordingly received permission, he set out.

La Roche Ferrière having gone, the thirty who got up the demonstration or supplicatory paper above referred to threw everything into disorder in the fort, of which they determined to take possession in order to effect a change in the conduct of affairs. As the best mode of proceeding, they chose as leaders one M. de Fourneaux, a great hypocrite, and excessively avaricious; one Stephen of Genoa, an Italian; and a third named La Croix: and of the soldiers a captain named Seignore, a Gascon. They then brought over to their way of thinking all the military officers except three: namely, M. d'Ottigny, the second in command; M. d'Arlac, the ensign, a Swiss gentleman; and Capt. La Caille. The rest of the soldiers they so effectually prevailed with, that sixty-six of them, being the best veteran men, joined them. They tried also to corrupt me, through some of my intimate friends, by showing me the list of names of those who had joined, and threatening terrible things against those who should not do the same. I, however, requested them not to trouble me further, as I was against them in this matter. M. de Laudonnière knew that some conspiracy was forming, but he did not know by whom. Some things also had come to the knowledge of M. d'Ottigny, but very obscurely. On the evening of the night during which the conspirators had decided to put their plan into execution, I was informed by a Norman gentleman named De Pompierre that they had resolved that night to cut the throat of Capt. La Caille, whose lodging and mine were the same; and that, if I valued my life, I had better be out of the way. As, however, the time was too short to allow me to make the necessary arrangements, I went home, and told La Caille what I had heard. He at once fled by a rear door, and hid himself in the woods; while I thought it best to recommend myself to the protection of God, and to await the event.

At midnight Fourneaux, the chief of the conspirators, armed with his cuirass, and carrying an arquebuse in his hand, and having twenty arquebusiers along with him, went to M. de Laudonnière's house, which he commanded to be opened; and, going straight to his bedside, put his weapon to his throat, and, assailing him with the vilest insults, seized the keys of the armory and storehouse, took away all his weapons, and, having put fetters on his feet, ordered him to be confined as a prisoner on the ship which lay in the river opposite the fort, under a guard of two soldiers. At the same time La Croix the other leader, also armed, and with fifteen men, entered the lodging of M. d'Ottigny, whom, however, they did not otherwise injure than to take away his arms, and forbid him, on pain of death, from leaving the house until daylight; which order he promised to obey. The same was done by Stephen the Genoese at the lodgings of the ensign, M. d'Arlac, who was obliged to take a similar oath. At the same time Capt. Seignore, with the rest of the soldiers who had joined the conspiracy, came to Capt. La Caille's, intending to kill him because he had openly opposed their undertaking after they had informed him of it; but, though they sought everywhere, they could neither find him nor his two brothers. They, however, carried away all their arms, as they also did mine; and an order was given that I should be carried a prisoner to the solders' quarters. At the intercession, however, of several gentlemen of high character, who, without any clear understanding of the affair, had been induced by others to go into it, my weapons were restored to me, on condition, however, that I should not leave the house until daylight; which I promised. He then went to the quarters of those soldiers who had not joined, and took possession of their arms; and thus the control of affairs was completely secured.

M. de Laudonnière being confined in chains as above related, his Lieutenant d'Ottigny, and his Ensign d'Arlac being disarmed and confined at home, Capt. La Caille being a wanderer among the wild beasts in the woods, and the rest of the true men being disarmed, the conspirators proceeded to upset the whole constitution of affairs, abusing, however, the name and authority of M. de Laudonnière, for the easier attaining of their objects. De Fourneaux, the chief of the conspiracy, caused a diploma or license to be drawn out on parchment, in the name of M. de Laudonnière, in which, as lieutenant of the king of France, he authorized the greater part of his force, in consequence of the scarcity of provisions, to proceed to New Spain to obtain supplies, and requesting all governors, captains, and others holding any office under the king of Spain, to aid them in this business. This document, which they themselves drafted, they forced M. de Laudonnière to sign. They then fitted out the two shallops that were before mentioned, taking the requisite armament and provisions from the king's stores, and selected the pilots and crews for the voyage to New Spain. They made the old man Michael Le Vasseur of Dieppe pilot of one, appointing to the other one Trenchant; and, thus prepared, they set sail from Carolina on the 8th December, calling us cowards and green hands, and threatening that if, on their return from New Spain with the wealth they proposed to acquire, we should refuse to admit them into the fort, they would tread us under foot.

But, while these are in the pursuit of wealth by piracy, let us return to La Roche Ferrière, who, having reached the mountains, succeeded by prudence and assiduity in placing himself on a friendly footing with the three chiefs before mentioned, the most bitter enemies of King Outina. He was astonished at their civilization and opulence, and sent to M. de Laudonnière at the fort many gifts which they bestowed upon him. Among these were circular plates of gold and silver as large as a moderate-sized platter, such as they are accustomed to wear to protect the back and breast in war; much gold alloyed with brass, and silver not thoroughly smelted. He sent also some quivers covered with very choice skins, with golden heads to all the arrows; and many pieces of a stuff made of feathers, and most skilfully ornamented with rushes of different colors; also green and blue stones,

101

which some thought to be emeralds and sapphires, in the form of wedges, and which they used instead of axes, for cutting wood. M. de Laudonnière sent in return such commodities as he had, such as some thick rough cloths, a few axes and saws, and other cheap Parisian goods, with which they were perfectly satisfied.

By these dealings M. la Roche Ferrière brought himself into the worst possible odor with King Outina, and still more among his subordinate chiefs, who conceived such a hatred for him that they would not even call him by name, saying always, instead, "Timogua," that is, Enemy. As long, however, as La Roche Ferrière preserved the friendship of the three chiefs, he was able to go to and from the fort by other roads, as there are many small streams which empty into the River of May for fifteen or sixteen miles below the territory of King Outina.

I believe I shall not depart too far from my story if I mention a certain soldier who was emulous of the example of La Roche Ferrière, and therefore demanded permission from M. de Laudonnière to trade in another quarter. He was given it, but was warned to consider well what he was about, as it was not impossible that his attempt to open a trade would cost him his life; which, indeed, is what actually happened. This soldier was named Pierre Gambré, and was a young, strong, and active man, who had from early youth been brought up in the home of the Admiral de Châtillon. Having received his permission, he departed alone, without any servant, from the fort, laden with a parcel of cheap goods, and with his arquebuse, and began to trade up and down the country. He was so successful in his management, that he even came to exercise a sort of authority over the natives, whom he used to make bring his messages to us. At length, having visited a certain inferior chief called Adelano, who lived on a small island in the river, he became so friendly with him, and so great a favorite, that the chief gave him his daughter to wife. Although thus honored, he continued his pursuit of gain. In the chief's absence, he exercised authority in his stead, and did it so tyrannically, requiring the Indians to obtain for him things quite out of their power, that he made himself hated by all of them. But, as he was beloved by the chief, none ventured to complain. It happened at length, that he asked leave of the chief to make a visit to the fort, as he had not seen his friends there for twelve months. He received permission, but on condition that he should return in a few days. Having got together all his wealth, and embarked it in a canoe or skiff which was furnished him for the purpose, and with two Indians to paddle, he took leave of the chief. While on the journey, one of his companions recalled to mind that he had been, on a former occasion, beaten with sticks by this soldier; and, the booty now offering being an additional temptation, he concluded that so eligible an opportunity of securing at once revenge and plunder must not be missed. Accordingly, while the soldier was bending over a fire in complete security, the Indian seized an axe which lay next his victim, and split open his head. Then, seizing the goods, he and his companion fled.

I will now return to the liberation of M. de Laudonnière, and to the account of what took place after the departure of our men; who, by the way, had carried off with them certain half-casks of rich Spanish wine, which, as both M. de Laudonnière and his maid-servant asserted, had been put aside for the use of the sick. Capt. La Caille, who was wandering in the woods, learned from his younger brother, who had been acting as a messenger to keep him supplied with what his friends could furnish, of the departure of the men who had threatened his life, and at once came back to the fort. Here he set about encouraging the rest; exhorted all to take possession of their arms again (those who had gone not having had any use for them); and M. de Laudonnière was brought ashore from the ship, and his Lieutenant d'Ottigny and Ensign d'Arlac were safely let out of their homes. The muster-roll was called; all took oath anew, both of allegiance to the king, and of resistance to the enemy, in whose number those were now reckoned who had treated us so wickedly and contemptuously. Four captains were appointed; the whole company was divided into four companies under them, and so all returned to their regular duties.

While all this was taking place, there came to the fort a young gentleman of Poitiers, named De Groutaut, sent by M. La Roche Ferrière, one of whose companions he had always been, even during his expedition to the three kings near the Apalatcy Mountains. He brought word to M. de Laudonnière, that one of these three chiefs was taken with a great affection for the Christians; that he was powerful and wealthy, having always on foot a military force of four thousand men; and that he had requested M. La Roche Ferrière to signify to M. de Laudonnière that he offered to conclude a perpetual league with him; and that, as he understood that we were searching for gold, he would bind himself by any conditions we might require; that, if a hundred arquebusiers should be supplied him, he would certainly render them victorious masters of the Apalatcy Mountains. La Roche Ferrière, knowing nothing of the troubles at the fort, had promised that this should be arranged; nor is there any doubt that, had we not been so shamefully deserted by the greater part of our men, the experiment would have been tried, on the information of the remarkable liking which this chief had conceived for us. But M. de Laudonnière, considering that if he should send away a hundred men, he would not have force enough left to defend the post, deferred the expedition until reenforcements should arrive from France; and at the same time he did not feel entire confidence in the Indians, particularly since the time when he was cautioned on the subject by the Spaniards. It will not be foreign to my purpose to insert here something on this point, taken from the "History of Florida," written and published by M. de Laudonnière.

"While" (says he) "the Indians were visiting me, always bringing some gift or other, as fishes, deer, turkeys, leopards, bear's whelps, and other productions of the country, I, on my part, compensated them with hatchets, knives, glass beads, combs, and mirrors. Two Indians came one day to salute me in the name of their king, Marracon, who lived about forty miles southward from the fort. They informed me that there was living in the family of King Onachaquara a person called The Bearded; and that there was another with King Mathïaca, whose name they did not know, both foreigners. It occurred to me that these men might be Christians; and I therefore sent notice to all the chiefs in the vicinity, that if they had any Christians in their power, if they would bring them in to me,

I would reward them double. Under this inducement, such efforts were made that both the persons referred to were brought to me at the fort. They were naked, and their hair hung down to their hams, in the Indian fashion. They were Spaniards by birth, but had become so accustomed to the manners of the natives that at first our ways seemed to them like those of foreigners. After talking with them I gave them some clothes, and directed their hair to be cut. This was done; but they kept it, putting it up in cotton cloth, saying that they would carry it back home with them as a testimony of the hardships which they had experienced in India. In the hair of one of them was found hidden a bit of gold, worth about twenty-five crowns, which he gave me. On my inquiring about the countries they had travelled through, and how they had made their way to this province, they replied that about fifteen years before, three ships, aboard one of which they were, had been cast away near Calos, on the rocks called The Martyrs; that King Calos had saved and kept for himself the greater part of the riches with which these ships were laden; that such efforts were made that the greater part of the crew were saved, as were many women, of whom three or four were noble ladies, married, and who with their children were still living with this King Calos. On being asked who this king was, they said he was the handsomest and largest Indian of all that region, and an energetic and powerful ruler. They also reported that he possessed a great store of gold and silver, and that he kept it in a certain village in a pit not less than a man's height in depth, and as large as a cask; and that, if I could make my way to that place with a hundred arquebusiers, they could put all that wealth into my hands besides what I might obtain from the richer of the natives. They said further, that, when the women met for the purpose of dancing, they wore, hanging at their girdles, flat plates of gold as large as quoits, and in such numbers that the weight fatigued and inconvenienced them in dancing; and that the men were similarly loaded. The greater part of all this wealth, they were of opinion, came from Spanish ships, of which numbers are wrecked in that strait; the rest from the trade between the king and the other chiefs in the neighborhood. That this king was held in great veneration by his subjects, whom he had made to believe that it was owing to his magical incantations that the earth afforded them the necessaries of life. The better to maintain this belief, he was accustomed to shut himself up along with two or three confidential persons in a certain building, where he performed these incantations; and any one inquisitive enough to try to see what was going on was at once killed by the king's orders. They added, that every year at harvest time, this barbarous king sacrificed a man who had been set apart expressly for this purpose, and who was chosen from among the Spaniards wrecked in the strait. One of them also told how he had for a long time acted as a courier to this chief, and had often been sent by him to a certain chief named Oathkaqua, who lived four or five days' journey from Calos, and had always been his faithful ally. Midway on this journey there is, in a great fresh-water lake called Sarrope, an island about five miles across, abounding in many kinds of fruit, and especially in dates growing on palm-trees, in which there is a great trade. There is a still greater one in a certain root of which flour is made, of so good a quality that the most excellent bread is made of it, and furnished to all the country for fifteen miles round. Hence the inhabitants of this island gain great wealth from their neighbors, for they will not sell the root except at a high price. Moreover, they are reckoned the bravest of all that region, as they showed by their actions when, King Calos having allied himself to King Oathkaqua by taking the daughter of the latter in marriage, she was taken prisoner after the betrothal. The account of this was as follows:--

"Oathkaqua, accompanied by a great number of his people, had brought to King Calos one of his daughters, a person of great beauty of form, and of an unusually lovely complexion, to give her to him in marriage. When the people of this island found this out, they laid an ambush for Oathkaqua;

and, attacking and routing him, they captured the bride and all her women, and carried them off to their island. This is reckoned by the Indians a peculiarly splendid victory; and they are accustomed to marry virgins whom they take in this manner, and to be excessively in love with them.

"Calos is on a river forty or fifty miles beyond the promontory of Florida that looks toward the south; while Oathkaqua lives this side of the promontory to the north of it, at the place called in the maps Canaveral, 28 degrees from the equator.

"About the 25th of January, my neighbor Paracousi Saturioua sent me some presents by two of his men, and wanted to engage me to unite my force with his in an attack on Outina, a friend to me; and asking particularly that I would recall some of my men who were staying with Outina, and on whose account he had refrained from attacking and overthrowing Outina. A number of other chiefs, who had leagued themselves together, repeatedly sent messages to me to the same effect, during three weeks or a month. I was, however, disinclined to comply with this request; but, on the contrary, used all the means in my power to put them on friendly terms. They consented to this, and in a way which might justify me in supposing that they were disposed to consider any thing right which I might determine. It was now that both the Spaniards, whose long experience had familiarized them with the Indian character, cautioned me not to put any faith in them at all; for that, when their conduct was most engaging, it was most certain that they were plotting some treachery; and that they were by nature the most thorough traitors and deceivers. I had, however, already learned to distrust them; for my own experience, and the reading of recent accounts, had acquainted me with their thousand arts and frauds.

"The two shallops being now ready, I gave orders to Vasseur, in charge of one of them, to explore the seacoast towards the north, and to go as far as the river where Adusta is king; he being the chief from whose territory the French in the year 1562 procured supplies. I sent this chief two different suits of clothes, and some axes, knives, and other merchandise of small value, as a means of better obtaining his friendship. With the same object, I sent along with Vasseur a soldier named Aimon, who had been on the previous expedition to this chief, in hopes that he would remember him. And, before they embarked, I directed them to make careful inquiry what had happened to another soldier named Roussi, who had remained alone in that part of the country at the time when Nicolas Mallon, commanding a vessel, and the rest of his men concerned in the same previous expedition, embarked on their return to France. On their arrival our men learned that Roussi had been picked up and carried away by some vessel thereabouts; and I afterwards learned that this was a Spanish vessel on a coasting expedition, and that he had been carried to Havana in her. King Adusta sent back the shallop fully laden with maize and beans, besides two deer, two skins painted after their fashion, and some pearls,--of little value, however, as they had been exposed to fire; and he sent me word that he would give much land if I would settle in his territory, and that he had corn in store, and would give me as much as I wanted. At this time, there came, during seven weeks, so many pigeons, that we sometimes shot more than two hundred a day in the woods about the fort. When Vasseur returned, I sent a second expedition with two shallops, having soldiers and sailors aboard, with a present to be given in my name to the widow of a deceased chief named Hiouacara, who lived about twelve miles north of us. She received my men kindly, and loaded both the shallops for me with maize and nuts; and she sent in addition some baskets full of cassina leaves, of which they make a drink. The territory of this widow lady is said to produce the most and best quality of maize of any part of the seacoast. The same queen is reported to be the most beautiful of all the Indian women, and to stand in the highest esteem among them. Indeed, her subjects reverence her so much that they will not let her walk on the ground, but carry her about on their shoulders instead. Some days after she had thus sent me back my boats, she sent to me her hiatiqui, i.e., interpreter.

"As I now judged that I had provisions enough to last until ships should come from France, I sent my two shallops (that my men might not be idle) on an exploring expedition up the river, which they ascended thirty miles above Mathïaca, where they discovered a lake whose farther shore, as the Indians reported, could not be seen even from the tops of the tallest trees anywhere on this side. My men did not therefore attempt to go farther; but, coming back by way of Chilili, they discovered in the middle of the stream an island called Edelano, the most delightful of all islands in the world. Although only about three miles long and broad, it is most abounding in men and fruits. Between the town Edelano and the riverside, the road lay along a walk of three hundred paces long and fifteen wide, on either side of which were immense trees whose branches formed such an elegant vaulting overhead, that the work seemed not done by nature, but by art, and had perhaps not its like in the whole Christian world. At leaving this place, our men proceeded to Enecaque, then to Patchica, and then to Choya, where they left the shallops in a small branch of the river with some men as a guard, and made a visit to Outina, who received them most hospitably, and at their departure importuned them so urgently that six of them yielded to his requests, and remained with him;   among them a gentleman named *De Groutaut*. After remaining there two months, and diligently exploring the country, together with another person whom I had a good while before stationed there for the same purpose, M. de Groutaut returned to the fort, and reported that he had never seen a finer country. Among other accounts, he brought one of a region called *Oustaca*, which he had seen, whose king was so powerful that he could muster an army of three or four thousand Indians; to whom it was represented, if I would ally myself, we could together easily conquer all the rest; and, further, this king, I was informed, knew the road to the *Apalatcy Mountains*, which the French have been so eager to reach, and where the enemy of Oustaca resides; but that by joining forces we could easily overcome him. This chief sent me a flat piece of brass dug out of the mountains, from whose roots there rises a stream rich in gold, or as the Indians think it, brass. They are accustomed to gather up the sand of this stream into hollow reeds until they are full; when, by shaking the reeds about, they find grains of gold and silver; from which they conjecture that there is a vein of the metal within the mountains. Since, however, they were at least five or six days' journey from the fort at *Thracia*, I resolved, that, as soon as re-enforcements should reach me from France, I would transfer our establishment to some river farther north, where we should be nearer these mountains."

To return now to our gentlemen and soldiers who set out for *New Spain* after provisions. They went to *Cuba*, where they captured some vessels, in some cases with little difficulty, and laden with supplies of all kinds, such as cassava, olive-oil, and Spanish wine; and they took possession of these ships for their own purposes, leaving their own vessels. Not contented with this booty, they made descents upon several points in the island, carrying off enough plunder, as they reckoned, to come to two thousand crowns apiece. Afterwards they took, though not until after a fight, a swift vessel with great wealth on board, and with her the governor of a certain port in that island called *La Havana*. This official offered a great sum of money as a ransom for himself and his two children. The amount was agreed on, but there were required in addition four or six monkeys of the sort called saguins, which are very beautiful, and as many parrots, of which choice ones are found in that island; and the governor was to remain a prisoner on board the ship until the ransom should be paid. To all this he agreed, and suggested that it would be the quickest way to send one of his children to his wife with a letter explaining the terms. Our Frenchmen read this letter when he had written it, and, not seeing any thing

108

wrong in it, sent it to Havana, as suggested, in the boat of the ship. But, astute and cautious as they thought themselves, they had not heard a few words which the governor managed to whisper into his son's ear; to wit, that his wife was not to do at all as was set forth in the letter, but was to send post-riders to every port in the island, to summon assistance. So effectively did the lady obey these orders, that at daybreak next morning our ferocious Frenchmen found themselves beset by two large men-of-war, whose broadsides were ready to be opened upon them on either side, and another large vessel besides. Finding themselves thus trapped, as the entrance to the harbor where they lay was narrow, they were greatly cast down; but six and twenty of them threw themselves into a small fast-sailing vessel that was in the place, as she was less likely to be hit by the balls; and, cutting her cable, fought their way out through the enemy. All the rest, however, who remained on board the ship with the governor, were taken, and, except five or six who were killed in the affair, were carried off to the mainland, and thrown into prison. Part of them were afterwards sold as slaves, and taken to other places, even as far as to Spain and Portugal.

Among those who escaped, were the three chiefs of the conspiracy, Fourneaux, Stephen the Genoese, and La Croix. Trenchant the pilot, who had been forced to accompany them,

was also in this party, with five or six sailors. These finding their craft without provisions, and that there was no way of getting any, agreed with each other to take the vessel back to Florida while the rest were asleep, which they did. The military men, when they awoke, were very indignant, for they were afraid of M. de Laudonnière: however, they concluded that it was best to put in at the mouth of the River of May for provisions, as they knew many Indians from whom they could get supplies; after which they could put to sea again, and try their fortune, unknown to the garrison at the fort. Having accordingly reached the mouth of the river, they cast anchor, and began to search for provisions, when one of the Indians brought the news to M. de Laudonnière. On this, he was about to send them orders to bring the ship up opposite the fort, and appear before him; but Capt. La Caille begged him to proceed cautiously, as they might probably take to flight, instead of obeying, in which case the opportunity of making an example of them would be lost. "Well," said M. de Laudonnière, "what do you advise, then?"--"I beg you," answered La Caille, "to give me twenty-five arquebusiers, whom I will stow in one of the shallops, and cover with her sail, and get up to their vessel at daybreak. If they see only two or three of us, and a couple of hands managing the shallop, they will not object to our coming alongside; and, when we are close to them, my men shall spring up, and board them." This plan was agreed to: the soldiers went on board; and when, next morning before daylight, the watch on board the other ship got sight of the boat, they called all hands. When, however, they recognized at some distance, on board the boat, only La Caille and a couple of men, they allowed them to come alongside without preparing to defend themselves. As soon as the boat was made fast to the vessel, however, our men sprang suddenly up, and boarded her. Surprised, they called out to fire on them, and ran to arms. But it was too late: they were quickly deprived of their weapons, and told that they were to be brought before the king's lieutenant; which put them into consternation enough, as they felt that their lives were in the greatest danger. They were taken to the fort, and the three principal conspirators were regularly tried, condemned, and punished, while the rest being, however, discharged from the service, were pardoned; and there were no further seditions.

After this affair was settled, there was a great scarcity with us, because for various reasons the Indians, both those nearby and those farther off, all broke off their intercourse with us. One of these reasons was, that they obtained nothing from us in exchange for their provisions; another, that they suffered much violence from our men in their expeditions after supplies. Some were even senseless, not to say malignant, enough to burn their houses, with the notion that by so doing we should be more promptly supplied. But the difficulty daily increased, until we had to go three or four miles before we could meet a single Indian. Then there took place, moreover, a campaign against the powerful chief Outina, which I need not narrate, as an account of it is given in M. de Laudonnière's work. In short, a detailed description of the condition of want to which we were reduced would be pitiful; but the plan of my work requires me to be very summary in my accounts.

After, however, some of us had actually perished of hunger, and all the rest were starved until our skin cleaved to our bones, M. de Laudonnière at last gave up hopes of receiving re-enforcements from France, for which he had now been waiting eighteen months, and called a general council to deliberate on the means of returning to France. It was herein finally concluded to refit as well as possible the third of our ships, and to raise her sides with plank so as to enlarge her capacity; and, while the artificers were employed on this work, the soldiers were set to collect provisions along the coast.

While we were busily employed in this matter, however, a certain English commander named Hawkins, who was returning home from a long voyage, came up to our fort in his boat; and, on observing our miserable condition, offered us any assistance in his power, and proceeded at once to make his offers good; for he sold to M. de Laudonnière one of his ships at a very moderate price, together with some casks of flour which we baked into biscuits. He also gave us several casks of beans and pease, and accepted as part payment in advance some of our brass cannon, and then proceeded on his voyage.

We were rejoiced enough at thus getting possession of another vessel besides our own, which was being repaired, and of sufficient provisions for our return; and on consultation it was decided that before our departure the fort should be destroyed: in the first place, to prevent its being made serviceable against the French, in case of their ever returning into those parts, by the Spaniards, who as we knew were desirous of establishing themselves there; and, secondly, to prevent Saturioua from occupying it. So we destroyed the works.

After, however, we were quite ready for the voyage, and when we had been for three weeks only waiting for a fair wind to depart from the province, there unexpectedly arrived a fleet of seven ships, commanded by the famous Jean de Ribaud, well known for his great merits, and who was sent out to succeed M. de Laudonnière, and for the carrying-on of the king's designs. This arrival, so wholly unexpected, filled us all with joy. M. de Ribaud landed with a number of his officers and many gentlemen and others. They all thanked God, while they were administering to our necessities, that they found us alive, for they had been informed that we had all perished; and so, after the long affliction which we had endured, God sent us happiness. All the new-comers individually were liberal in imparting food and whatever else they had brought, and tried in every way to be serviceable each to such friends or kinsmen or fellow-countrymen as he met with among us: so all the place was filled with happiness. But this joy was brief, as we quickly found.

M. de Ribaud desiring to land his treasure, provisions, and military supplies, had the mouth of the river sounded; but, finding too little water for his larger vessels, he ordered the three smaller ones only into the river. One of these, "The Pearl," was commanded by his son Jacques de Ribaud, to whom Capt. Vallard of Dieppe acted as lieutenant; Capt. Maillard, also of Dieppe, commanded the second; and the captain of the third was a gentleman named Machonville. The four larger ships remained at anchor a mile from the shore, as the water was shallow there, and were unloaded by canoes and boats.

Seven or eight days after Ribaud's arrival, while all the gentlemen, soldiers, and sailors, except a few men left in charge of the four larger ships, were on shore, and occupied about putting up houses, and rebuilding the fort, about four o'clock in the afternoon some soldiers who were walking on the seashore saw six ships steering towards our four which were at anchor. They instantly sent information to Ribaud; and upon his coming up, rather late, they told him that these six large ships had cast anchor near ours, which had at once cut their cables, and gone to sea under all sail; that the six had thereupon weighed anchor, and sailed in pursuit. Ribaud, indeed, and many others with him, were in season to see this chase with their own eyes. Our ships, however, being faster than the others, were quickly out of sight, and within a quarter of an hour the pursuers had also disappeared. This made us uneasy enough all the following night, during which Ribaud ordered all the small craft to be made ready, and stationed five or six hundred arquebusiers on the shore, in readiness to embark if needed. Thus the night passed away, and the next day until about noon, when the largest of our four ships, "The Trinity," came in sight, steering directly for us. Soon we saw the second, under Capt. Cossette, then the third, and a little afterwards the fourth; and they signalled us to come on board. But Ribaud fearing that the enemy might have taken the ships, and were trying to trap us, would not risk his men, eager though they were to go aboard. As the wind was adverse, and the ships could not come in close, Capt. Cossette wrote a letter to Ribaud, which one of his sailors took, and, jumping into the sea at the imminent risk of his life, swam for shore. After swimming a long distance, he was seen from the land, and a boat put out, picked him up, and brought him to Ribaud. The letter was as follows:--

"M. De Ribaud,--Yesterday at four, P.M., a Spanish fleet of eight ships hove in sight, six of which cast anchor near us. Seeing that they were Spaniards, we cut cables, and made sail; and they immediately made sail in chase, and pursued us all night, firing many guns at us. Finding, however, that they could not come up with us, they have made a landing five or six miles below, putting on shore a great number of negroes with spades and mattocks. On this state of facts, please to act as you shall see fit."

On reading this letter, Ribaud at once called a council of his chief subordinates, including nearly thirty military officers, besides gentlemen, commissaries, and other civilians. The more prudent part of this assembly would have preferred to complete the erection and arming of the fort as soon as possible, while Laudonnière's men, who knew the country, should be sent against the Spaniards; a plan which, God willing, would, they thought, quickly settle matters, since the locality was not within the Spanish jurisdiction, whose limits, indeed, were three or four hundred miles distant. Ribaud, however, after perceiving this plan to be generally acceptable, said, "Gentlemen, I have heard your views, and desire now to state my own. First, however, you should be informed that, a little before our leaving France, I received a letter from the admiral, at the end of which he had written with his own hand as follows: 'M. de Ribaud, we have advices that the Spaniard means to attack you. Do not yield a particle to him, and you will do right.' I must therefore declare plainly to you that it may result from your plan that the Spaniards will not await an assault from our brave men, but will at once escape aboard ship, by which we should lose our opportunity of destroying those who are seeking to destroy us. The better plan seems to me to be, to put all our soldiers on board our four ships now at anchor, and to seize at once upon their ships, while anchored where they have landed. When those are taken they will have no refuge except the works which their slaves have been throwing up; and we can then attack them by land to much better advantage."

M. de Laudonnière, who was by this time familiar with the climate of the country, now suggested that the weather should be carefully taken into account before putting the men on board ship again; as at that time of year a species of whirlwinds or typhoons, which sailors call "houragans," from time to time come on suddenly, and inflict terrible damage on the coast. For this reason he favored the former of the proposed plans; the rest, for the same and other reasons, have already been described as of the like mind. Ribaud alone, however, contemning all their reasons, persisted in his own determination, which was no doubt the will of God, who chose this means of punishing his own children, and destroying the wicked. Not satisfied with his own force, M. de Ribaud asked for Laudonnière's captains and his ensign, whom the latter could not well refuse to send with him; and all Laudonnière's men, when they saw their standard-bearer going, insisted on going with him. I myself, seeing them all going, went on board with the rest, though lame in one leg, and not yet recovered from a wound I had received in the campaign against Outina.

All the troops being now on board, a fair wind for an hour or two was all that was needed to bring us up with the enemy; but just as the anchors were about to be weighed the wind changed, and blew directly against us, exactly from the point where the enemy were, for two whole days and nights, while we waited for it to become fair. On the third day, as signs of a change appeared, Ribaud ordered all the officers to inspect their men; and M. d'Ottigny finding in his examination of Laudonnière's force, that I was not yet quite cured, had me put into a boat along with another soldier, a tailor by trade, who was at work on some clothes for him against the proposed return to France, and sent us, against our wills, back to the fort. But just as they had weighed anchor, and set sail, there came up all at once so terrible a tempest that the ships had to put out to sea as quickly as possible for their own safety; and, the storm continuing, they were driven to the northward some fifty miles from the fort, where they were all wrecked on some rocks, and destroyed. All the ships' companies were, however, saved except Capt. La Grange, a gentleman of the house of the Admiral de Châtillon, a man of much experience and many excellencies, who was drowned. The Spanish ships were also wrecked and destroyed in the same gale.

As the storm continued, the Spaniards, who were informed of the embarkation of the French forces, suspected, what was not so very far from the truth, that the troops had been cast away and destroyed in it, and fancied that they could easily take our fort. Although the rains continued as constant and heavy as if the world was to be again overwhelmed with a flood, they set out, and marched all night towards us. On our part, those few who were able to bear arms were that same night on guard; for, out of about a hundred and fifty persons remaining in the fort, there were scarcely twenty in a serviceable condition, since Ribaud, as before mentioned, had carried off with him all the able soldiers except fourteen or fifteen who were sick or mutilated, or wounded in the campaign against Outina. All the rest were either servants or mechanics who had never even heard a gun fired, or king's commissaries better able to handle a pen than a sword; and, besides, there were some women, whose husbands, most of them, had gone on board the ships. M. de Laudonnière himself was sick in bed.

When the day broke, nobody being seen about the fort, M. de la Vigne, who was the officer of the guard, pitying the drenched and exhausted condition of the men, who were worn out with long watching, permitted them to take a little rest; but they had scarcely had time to go to their quarters, and lay aside their arms, when the Spaniards, guided by a Frenchman named François Jean, who had seduced some of his messmates along with him, attacked the fort at the double quick in three places at once, penetrated the works without resistance, and, getting possession of the place of arms, drew up their force there. Then parties searched the soldiers' quarters, killing all whom they found, so that awful outcries and groans arose from those who were being slaughtered. For my own part, whenever I call to mind the great wonder that God, to whom truly nothing is impossible, brought to pass in my case, I cannot be enough astonished at it, and am, as it were, stunned with the recollection. On coming in from my watch, I laid down my arquebuse; and, all wet through as I was, I threw myself into a hammock which I had slung up after the Brazilian fashion, hoping to get a little sleep. But on hearing the outcries, the noise of weapons, and the sound of blows, I jumped up again, and was going out of the house to see what was the matter, when I met in the very doorway two Spaniards with their swords drawn, who passed on into the house without accosting me, although I brushed against them. When, however, I saw that nothing was visible except slaughter, and that the place of arms itself was held by the Spaniards, I turned back at once, and made for one of the embrasures, where I knew I could get out. At the very place I found five or six of my fellow-soldiers lying dead, among whom were two that I recognized, La Gaule and Jean du Den. I leaped down into the ditch, crossed it, and went on alone for some distance over rising ground into a piece of woods, until, having reached a higher part of the hill, it was as if God gave me back my consciousness; for it is certain that the things that had happened since my leaving the house were as though I had been out of my wits. I now prayed God for his guidance in my actions, in this so extreme danger; and, at a suggestion from his Spirit,

went forward into the woods, whose paths, by frequent use of them, I well knew. I had gone but a little way when, to my great joy, I came upon four other Frenchmen; and, after condoling with each other, we consulted on what to do next. Part of us advised to stay where we were until next day, when perhaps the fury of the Spaniards would be appeased; and then to return, and surrender ourselves to them, rather than risk being devoured by wild beasts where we were, or perishing by hunger of which we had already endured so much. Some of the rest, not liking these suggestions, thought it a better plan to make our way to some distant Indian settlement, where we might live until God should open some way for us. But I said, "Brothers, I like neither of these suggestions. If you will be guided by me, we will make for the seashore through the woods, and try if we cannot discover something of the two small vessels which Ribaud sent into the river to be used in disembarking the provisions he brought from France." But, this appearing to them perfectly impracticable, they set off to find the Indians, leaving me alone. But God, taking pity on my distress, sent me another companion, being Grandchemin, that very soldier whom M. d'Ottigny sent back with me to the fort to work on some clothes for him. I suggested to him the same as to the others, that is, to endeavor to find the two small craft at the seashore. He thought well of this, and we were all that day on the road before we got through the woods. Before we could reach the shore, however, we had extensive swamps to pass, all thickly grown with large reeds, very hard to get through. With all this toil we were pretty well exhausted when night fell, and a steady rain began also to come down upon us. The tide likewise rose in the swamp until the water there among the reeds was over our waists; and we spent the whole night in working our way onward under these difficulties. When the daylight came, and we could see nothing in the direction of the sea, the soldier, losing his patience, said it would be better to surrender ourselves to the enemy, and that we might as well return to them; that, when they found that we were artificers, they would spare our lives; and, even if they should not, was it not better to let them kill us than to remain any longer in such a miserable condition? I sought to dissuade him, but in vain; and, as I saw that he was about to leave me, I finally promised to go back with him to the Spaniards. We therefore made our way back through the woods, and were even in sight of the fort, when I heard the uproar and rejoicing which the Spaniards were making, and was deeply moved by it, and said to the soldier, "Friend and companion, I pray you, let us not go thither: let us stay away yet a little while; God will open some way of safety to us, for he has many of which we know nothing, and will save us out of all these dangers." But he embraced me, saying, "I will go: so farewell." In order to see what should happen to him, I got up to a height near by, and watched. As he came down from the high ground, the Spaniards saw him, and sent out a party. As they came up to him, he fell on his knees to beg for his life. They, however, in a fury cut him to pieces, and carried off the dismembered fragments of his body on the points of their spears and pikes. I hid myself again in the woods, where, having gone about a mile, I came upon a Frenchman of Rouen, La Crète by name, a Belgian called Elie des Planques, and M. de Laudonnière's maid-servant, who had been wounded in the breast. We made our way towards the open meadows along the seashore; but before getting through the woods, we found M. de Laudonnière himself, and another man named Bartholomew, who had received a deep sword-cut in the neck; and after a time we picked up others, until there were fourteen or fifteen of us in all. As, however, a carpenter called Le Chaleux, who was one of us, has given a brief account of this part of our calamities, I will say nothing more except that we travelled in water more than waist-deep for two days and two nights through swamps and reeds; M. de Laudonnière, who was a skilful swimmer, and the young man from Rouen, swimming three large rivers on the way, before we could get sight of the two vessels. On the third day, by the blessing of God, and with the help of the sailors, we got safe on board.

I have already mentioned, that, as Ribaud found that there was not water enough at the mouth of the river to admit his four largest vessels, he had sent in his three smaller ones, which he purposed to use in discharging the others; his son Jacques de Ribaud being in command of the largest of the three. He had taken his vessel up to the fort, and lay there at anchor while the Spaniards were perpetrating their butchery; nor, although he had cannon, did he once fire upon them. All that day the wind was contrary, and prevented him from getting the ship out of the river. The Spaniards in the mean time offered him good terms and amnesty if he would surrender, to which he made no reply. When they saw that he was trying persistently to get his ship out to sea, they took a small boat which was used at the fort, and sent her on board of him with a trumpeter, and that same traitor, Francois Jean, who had guided the Spaniards into the fort, to request a parley to arrange terms of agreement. And, although this traitor was reckless enough to even venture himself aboard of the ship of Jacques de Ribaud, the latter was so imbecile and timid as not to venture to detain him, but let him go safe back again, although he had on board, besides his crew, more than sixty soldiers. But, on the other hand, neither did

the Spaniards, although they had abundance of small boats, dare to make any attacks upon him.

On the next day, however, Jacques got his ship to the mouth of the river, where he found the other two smaller vessels nearly emptied of men; for the greater and better part of them had gone with Jean de Ribaud. Laudonnière therefore decided to fit out and man one of the two with the armament and crews of both; and then advised with Jacques what they should do, and whether they ought not to search for his father; to which the latter made answer that he wanted to go back to France, which was in the end resolved upon. First, however, as there was no provision except biscuit in the smaller vessel, and she was without water, Laudonnière had some empty casks filled with water, and Jacques did the like. In this, and in obtaining some other necessary supplies, two days were consumed, during all which time the ships were kept close side by side, for fear the Spaniards might attack us, as their boats reconnoitered us from time to time, not, however, venturing within gunshot distance. Certainly, as we knew what actions they had perpetrated upon our friends, we were prepared to make a desperate defence.

Before sailing, Laudonnière asked Jacques de Ribaud to accommodate him with one of his four pilots, as he had no skilful navigator on board, but was refused. He then further observed that it would be well to sink our vessels left at the mouth of the river, lest the Spaniards should get possession of them, and use them to prevent Jean de Ribaud from entering the river, should he return and wish to do so (for we were ignorant of his shipwreck); but Jacques would consent to nothing. Laudonnière, finding him so obstinate, sent his own ship-carpenter, who scuttled and sunk the ships in question; namely, one which we had brought from France, one which we had bought of the English commander Hawkins, and one the smallest of M. de Ribaud's fleet; and, this done, we set sail from Florida, ill manned and ill provisioned. But God, however, gave us so fortunate a voyage, although attended with a good deal of suffering, that we made the land in that arm of the sea bordering on England which is called St. George's Channel.

This is what I have thought it proper to relate of the things which I witnessed on this voyage; from which it appears that victory is not of man, but of God, who does all things righteously according to his own will. For, according to all human judgment, fifty of the worst of Ribaud's soldiers could have destroyed all the Spanish force, of whom many were beggars and the dregs of the people; while Ribaud had more than eight hundred brave veteran arquebusiers, with gilded armor. But,

when such things are God's pleasure, it is for us to say, Blessed be the name of God everlasting!

As for the fate of Ribaud after his shipwreck, as I was not present with him, I can only relate what I heard from a sailor of Dieppe, who escaped from the Spaniards, as will be mentioned: I will therefore add a short statement of the facts. Having called the roll, and, as I have already mentioned, having found all present except Capt. La Grange, although all their weapons had been lost in the wreck, Ribaud made a noble speech to his men, setting forth that it was their duty to bear with calmness the calamity which they had suffered by the will of God; for he was a man of piety, and a fine speaker. Prayers having then been offered, it was decided to set out for the fort, from which they were about fifty miles away. In this march they must unquestionably have undergone great hardships, and made great exertions; for the region through which they had to travel was much intersected by rivers, and was neither inhabited by the Indians, nor cultivated at all; so that they had to live on roots and herbs, and were sufficiently anxious in their minds. Having, however, courageously made their way through all obstacles, they finally reached a point some four or five miles, as well as the soldiers from Laudonnière's force could judge, from the fort. Ribaud now determined not to advance any nearer, but called a council to deliberate on what should be done. The conclusion was, to send Vasseur, a skilful seaman, and who knew all the branches of the River of May, with five or six men, in an Indian canoe, to reconnoitre, and ascertain something about the Frenchmen who had been left in the fort. Upon going down the river to the neighborhood of the fort, he saw the Spanish flag flying over it; and, returning without being observed by the garrison, he made report to Ribaud. Upon hearing the story, it may easily be imagined how great was the grief of Ribaud and all his company, and how utterly he was at a loss what to say or do. For his own part, he foresaw the cruelty of the Spaniards; and yet he perceived that most of his force would perish by starvation and exposure in the woods; but, before resolving on any definite step, it was decided to send some messenger to the fort, to learn something of the intentions of the Spaniards, and what disposal had been made of the Frenchmen left in the fort. For this purpose were sent Nicolas Verdier, captain of one of the ships, and La Caille, that officer of Laudonnière's of whom mention has already been made. They went in a canoe with five or six soldiers, and, according to orders, showed themselves at a good distance off. The Spaniards, on seeing them, came in a boat to the other bank of the river, and held a parley with our men. The French asked what had become of the men left in the fort. The Spaniards replied that their commander, who was a humane and clement person, had sent them all to France in a large ship abundantly supplied, and that they might say to Ribaud that he and his men should be used equally well. The French returned with this message. Ribaud, on hearing it, believed too hastily this story about his men having been sent back to France, and summoned another council. Here most of the soldiers began at once to cry out, "Let us go, let us go! What is to hinder our going over to them at once? Even if they should put us to death, is it not better to die outright than to endure so many miseries? There is not one of us who has not experienced a hundred deaths while we have been making this journey!" Others, more prudent, said they could never put faith in Spaniards; for, they urged, if there were no other reason than the hatred which they bear to us on account of our religion, they assuredly will not spare us.

Ribaud, however, perceiving that most were of his mind, that it was best to surrender to the Spaniards, decided to send La Caille in to the Spanish commander, with orders, if the latter should seem inclined to clemency, to ask, in the name of the lieutenant of the king of France, for a safe-conduct, and to announce, that, if the Spanish leader would make oath to spare all their lives, they would come in, and throw themselves at his feet. The greater part of the company assented to this, and La Caille was accordingly sent; who, coming to the fort, was taken before the commander, and, throwing himself at his feet, delivered his message. Having heard La Caille through, he not only pledged his faith to La Caille in the terms suggested, and confirmed the pledge with many signs of the cross, and by kissing the Evangelists, but made oath in the presence of all his men, and drew up a writing sealed with his seal, repeating the oath, and promising that he would without fraud, faithfully, and like a gentleman and a man of honesty, preserve the lives of Ribaud and his men. All this was handsomely written out, and given to La Caille; but this fine paper promise was worth just as much as the blank paper. La Caille, however, took back this elegant document with him; which was joyfully received by some, while others did not entertain any great expectations from it.

Ribaud, however, having made an excellent speech to his people, and all having joined in offering prayer to God, gave orders to proceed, and with all his company came down to the bank of the river near the fort. Upon being seen by the Spanish sentinels, they were taken over in boats. Ribaud himself, and D'Ottigny, Laudonnière's lieutenant, were first led into the fort by themselves; the rest were halted about a bowshot from the fort, and were all tied up in fours, back to back; from which, and other indications, they quickly perceived that their lives were lost. Ribaud asked to see the governor, to remind him of his promise; but he spoke to deaf ears. D'Ottigny, hearing the despairing cries of his men, appealed to the oath which had been taken, but they laughed at him. As Ribaud insisted on his application, a Spanish soldier finally came in, and asked in French if he were the commander, "Ribaut." The answer was, "Yes." The man asked again, if Ribaud did not expect, when he gave an order to his soldiers, that they would obey; to which he said again, "Yes."--"I propose to obey the orders of my commander also," replied the Spaniard; "I am ordered to kill you"; and with that he thrust a dagger into his breast; and he killed D'Ottigny in the same way. When this was done, men were detailed to kill all the rest who had been tied up, by knocking them in the head with clubs and axes; which they proceeded to do without delay, calling them meanwhile Lutherans, and enemies to God and to the Virgin Mary. In this manner they were all most cruelly murdered in violation of an oath, except a drummer from Dieppe named Dronet, a fifer, and another man from Dieppe, a fiddler named Masselin, who were kept alive to play for dancing; and one sailor escaped in the following manner, being the same who related to me this narrative:--

He was among those who were pinioned for slaughter, and was knocked in the head with the rest, but, instead of being killed, was only stunned; and, the three others with whom he was tied falling above him, he was left for dead along with them. The Spaniards got together a great pile of wood to burn the corpses; but, as it grew late, they put it off until the next day. The sailor, coming to his senses among the dead bodies in the night, bethought himself of a knife which he wore in a wooden sheath, and contrived to work himself about until little by little he got the knife out, and cut the ropes that bound him. He then rose up, and silently departed, journeying all the rest of the night. When the day broke, he laid his course by the sun to get as far away from the fort as possible (for those of maritime occupations acquire the ability to judge which way they are going from observing where the sun is); and, after travelling for three days without stopping, he came to a certain Indian chief, who lived forty miles from the fort, with whom he remained hidden eight months, before he was betrayed to the Spaniards.

About eight months after their capture of the fort, the Spaniards learned that some of the French had escaped, and were dispersed about the province. The Spanish commander, fearing that they would engage with the natives in some enterprise against him, sent threatening messages to the chiefs around, demanding the surrender of the French who were in hiding with them. The protector of this sailor, therefore, informed him that he must deliver himself to the Spaniards, as otherwise he feared he should be attacked, and his possessions burned. The sailor would have taken refuge with other chiefs; but they all answered him to the same effect. Not knowing what to do, he set out for the fort; but, having come within two miles of it, he could not resolve to go any farther, but stopped, and exhausted with sorrow, anxiety, and despair, gave himself over to die, and remained for three or four days in that miserable state. At the end of that time three Spaniards came out hunting, one of whom discovered him, and, at the sight of what was more like a dead corpse than a live man, felt (what is hardly to be found in one out of a thousand Spaniards) a sensation of pity upon beholding the sailor at his feet, and begging for mercy. Being asked by the Spaniard how he came to be there, he told him his story; upon which the Spaniard, who was affected by it, agreed that he would not take him at once to the fort, for fear of his being killed on the spot, but would see the governor first, and try if some indulgence could not be had from him; and that, after ascertaining about this, he would come back. Leaving him, therefore, the soldier went to the governor, and managed to get him to promise that the sailor need not be killed, but should only be made a slave. Next day he accordingly returned to the miserable Frenchman, and carried him to the fort, where he served as a slave for a year, and was then sent into Cuba, to Havana, where he was chained to another Frenchman, a gentleman called M. de Pompierre, who had been captured along with others of Laudonnière's men, after being carried off against his will on that expedition which I have already referred to in the course of this short account of the whole expedition. At last De Pompierre and the sailor were sold together, and put on board ship for Portugal; but the vessel happened to fall in with a French ship commanded by one Bontemps, and after a long fight was taken by her, when the victors, finding our two prisoners on board in chains, set them at liberty, and carried them to France. Thus God, according to his pleasure, finds ways to relieve the unfortunate even when they have lost all hope.

This is the story which I heard from the sailor of the destruction of Ribaud and his company; but it becomes us to accuse ourselves and our own sins for blame in the matter, and not the Spaniards, whom the Lord made use of as rods for scourging us according to our deserts. But to God omnipotent alone, and to his Son Jesus Christ our Lord, and to the Holy Spirit, be honor and glory forever! Amen.

The Letters

The Letters

Almost half a century of futile exploration and attempted settlement of Florida cost Spain the lives of Ponce de León, Narváez, De Soto, and many of her other citizens. The expensive colonization effort at Pensacola Bay, led by Tristán de Luna y Arellano, ended in controversy and failure. In 1561 Philip II seems to have concluded that the potential return from Florida did not justify further effort. At least he sought the counsel of Viceroy Don Luis de Velasco concerning a policy which would involve the abandonment of the vast region of North America lying above and east of the Rio Grande.

This hesitation of the Spanish monarch gave opportunity to ambitious France. Her famous naval captain, Jean Ribault, explored Florida in 1562 and left colonists at Port Royal. The civil war in France prevented Ribault from returning to his colony, and he sought aid in Great Britain. Meanwhile, a truce in France enabled Admiral Gaspard de Coligny, leader of the French Protestants, to send colonists to Florida. In 1564 René de Laudonnière established his Huguenot settlers at Fort Caroline on the south bank of the St. Johns River, not far from present-day Jacksonville.

The French settlement endangered the trade of Spain with her most productive colonies in the New World. Control of Florida and command of the Bahama Channel would enable France to attack the Spanish treasury fleets sailing from Mexico and Panama to Spain. The English Sea Dogs were also attacking Spanish commerce. These events which involved Spain, France, and England led to a settlement at St. Augustine, the oldest settlement by Europeans within the present area of the United States.

On SEPTEMBER 23, 1561, Philip II issued a royal order relating to Florida. After reciting the Spanish failures at Pensacola and Santa Elena, and negative information from Pedro Menéndez on the value of settlements north of New Spain (that is, in Florida), the paper commands the viceroy of New Spain to consult with others and forward a report so that the King may decide what it is best to do. The report of the Council of New Spain was dated March 12, 1562, and stated that the King's order was based on accurate information. The report—"Parecer que da a S.M. el Consejo de la Nueva España, en virtud de su Real Cédula (fecha en Madrid a 23 Septiembre de 1561) que sique, sobre la forma en que estava la costa de la Florida, y que no convenía aumentar la Población"—is in the Buckingham Smith Collection (New York Public Library), vol. 1561-1593, p. 11.

This translation of the king's order is in the A. M. Brooks Manuscripts at the Library of Congress.

Philip II to Don Luis Velasco

To Don Louis de Velasco, our Viceroy and Captain General of New Spain and President of the Royal Council: By reports which we have received from persons who have been in Florida, we have learned of the bad failures of our various expeditions, when Tristán de Ayellanos went there, as well as when Angel de Villafañe afterwards went to the coast and cape of Santa Elena. Considering that so much money has been expended in said expeditions and the poor results we have obtained; and also the poverty which is said to exist in that land, which even if populated would produce very little; and that even the populating of Santa Elena, which is considered dangerous, would be of no use because of its port having no good entrance; and further considering that there is no danger of the French setting foot on that land, much less taking possession of it; and other reasons explained to us showing that it is not sensible to expend any more money from our Treasury in populating that land, or in founding a town at Cape Santa Elena; and also because Pedro

Menéndez de Avilés, when he was here, said that is was not expedient to populate that coast of Florida nor to supply it from New Spain, nor convenient to establish a town at Cape Santa Elena, because it has no harbor but only a river of shallow water, and that even if there were a good harbor there the currents are so strong that they would render navigation very difficult, and that, in his opinion, harbors should be only looked for between the 38th degree of latitude and the new land, and that, in selecting a harbor, care should be taken to examine the land and coast, and to select the best and most suitable locality, and that this can be done with more facility from your area and at less expense; then, owing to the nature of the business and the fact that you are so well acquainted with all things relative to that Province, I have decided before taking any steps in the matter to hear your opinion and resolution on the same in order that after all is understood that the best judgment may be made.

So I command that as soon as you should see this letter

that you consult with the persons of experience in your land and ascertain their views in regard to whether it would be expedient to continue populating the said Florida, or not. And if you and they are of the opinion that the efforts should be continued, then in what manner and from what point would it be most convenient to do so in order that the wise thing may be done. As soon as you obtain this information, you will send us a statement of the same as well as of your own views on the matter, so that, in view of the information before us, we may decide what will be best and most conducive to the service of God, Our Lord, and our own.

At Madrid, the 23rd day of September in the year 1561

El Rey

By order of His Majesty, Francisco de Eraso

Charles IX to M. de Jarnac

FOLLOWING THE EXPEDITION of Jean Ribault to Florida in 1562 and the establishment in that year of Charlesfort on what is now Parris Island, South Carolina, Charles IX on January 16, 1563, wrote a letter newly discovered and never before published, which is now on display at the Fort Caroline National Memorial. The letter apparently refers to the Captain Bourdet who visited Fort Caroline in September, 1564.

To Monsieur de Jarnac, Knight of my order, captain of fifty armed men, and my lieutenant in the government of La Rochelle.

Monsieur de Jarnac, I am now writing to Captain Bourdet that he should promptly stir up Nicolas Symon and his companions, who have recently returned from Florida, so that we can learn from them how things are going over there; and for this reason: I have heard that Captain Bourdet wishes to take them back on the voyage he wants to make to Florida; and if it works out that way, I could not find out from them what I want to ask them about. For that reason, I pray you to see to it, and give orders that Captain Bourdet not fail to send them to me, wherever I may be, so that I can be clearly informed on the situation over there, which I would like to learn about from them. And I pray to God, Monsieur de Jarnac, to hold you in His holy and worthy care.

From Paris, January 16, 1563

Charles

(Countersigned) F. Robertet

129

Spanish ambassadors to Great Britain kept their king informed of Jean Ribault's activities in England and the proposed English expeditions to Florida. The reports are in Martin A. S. Hume (ed.), *Calendar of Letters and State Papers, 1558-1567,* Vol. I, pp. 322, 334, 337, 485, 488, 493, 495, 502, 536, and 551.

Letters from the Spanish Embassy

ive vessels are being fitted out here by private individuals, the principal of whom is a young gentleman called Thomas Stukeley who is going in command. The talk is that they are going on a voyage of discovery to Florida, where a certain Captain Jean Ribault of Dieppe went to some months ago, who now accompanies Stukeley. Out of the five ships one belongs to the Queen, two to Stukeley, one to Ribault, and one is chartered. They take 300 men and a great quantity of materials and artificers as well as plenty of artillery. Many people think that their object is to attack some of Your Majesty's ships on their voyage from the Indies. Some days since Stukeley sent to me to say that these people were sending him on a bad and knavish business, but that he would be with me and would show me how to play them a trick that would make a noise in the world. I sent to seek him several times, but he left London without telling me anything. They tell me he will embark in Bristol, and takes no more than 300 soldiers divided amongst the five ships. I am endeavoring to find out what is the truth about the business, although I expect really that they are bound for Florida, and that Stukeley's idea was to mutiny with the ships and to magnify his importance by telling me that they had commissioned him to do something prejudicial to your Majesty's expeditions, and that he lacked courage at last to say it, thinking probably that the relations between Your Majesty and the Queen were too tranquil for him to make such a proposal, or perhaps he was waiting for me to speak first. He is quite capable of doing this, and, so far as his position is concerned, a good deal more, but is not much to be trusted. I thought well to advise your Majesty of it in good time in order that such measures might be taken as appeared advisable.

London, June 19, 1563

recently wrote to your Majesty how Thomas Stukeley had left here on a voyage of discovery to a certain land called here Florida, and that on several occasions he had given me to understand that he wished to speak with me, and even declared that he was dissatisfied with the Queen and desired to serve your Majesty. He recently came and spoke with me just as he was sailing, and told me he was leaving the country discontentedly and almost desperately. He had embarked in the six ships all that remained of his property, more with the intention of going to serve your Majesty than with the idea of any profit he could gain in the discovery on which he was bound. He therefore desired that I would convey to your Majesty the desire and resources he had to serve your Majesty in these six well-found ships. I told him I could do as he asked me, but would be glad to know in what way he thought he could serve your Majesty. He answered in any way he was ordered, and when I saw that he was not to be drawn out any further I took leave of him,

thanking him for his good intentions. When he was bidding me good-bye he again pressed me to let your Majesty know how attached he was to your service, and was anxious that this should be done expeditiously in case he should arrive at any port in Spain or other dominions of your Majesty, as he was desirous of being known as an adherent of your Majesty and treated as such. I answered him that there was no reason to doubt that this would be done considering the friendship that existed between the English and your Majesty's subjects, always on condition that this expedition was not bound to any place enclosed by your Majesty's boundaries. He said that where he was going no one had ever been except some few Frenchmen a short time ago and, as I wished to know more exactly where the country was, he told me it was three days' journey from Cuba. I then pointed out to him that this could not be without injury to your Majesty's interests, as the place fell within your boundaries. This he would not understand, and I did not care to waste time over it as I saw he was ready to sail and his visit to me was nothing but cunning, thinking in this way to ensure himself from molestation on his voyage. He bears the royal standard which the Queen has presented him with although the ships do not belong to her, nor to him either except two; for the others are chartered from private persons. They are fitted out and armed perfectly, and my own opinion is that Stukeley is bent rather on committing some great robbery than discovering new lands. I cannot say that he is instructed to do so, but I can only believe that his voyage is in consequence of the determination (advised by me in recent letters) of the admiral of France in conjunction with the people who govern here to harass your Majesty's shipping and conquer on the ocean where they aim at being the strongest, and of course take steps to make themselves so. I think of speaking to the Queen about it, although I know full well what answer she will give me, the same as often before both in speech and writing. I am of opinion that the best thing to be done would be to attack these ships in force and punish them if it could be effected and, if not, to take up with this Stukeley and make some use of him, since he offers himself and will do what he says. He is quite ruined here and without

estate, and has always professed to be a servitor of your Majesty. Whatever the object be--good or gain--to let English and French establish themselves in places so close to your Majesty's provinces and boundaries, certainly appears to me to be a thing likely to cause injury in the long run. Stukeley sailed yesterday from the port of London with three of his vessels, and the other three await him at Plymouth, but he may probably be unable to get away from the coast finally for some time as several other French ships which he is to convoy have not had time to get ready.

Three of the French hostages here, believing that during the continuance of war their stay was not necessary, agreed to escape, but they captured them at Gravesend and Jean Ribault with them. The other hostage being so devoted to the new religion preferred to remain here rather than go in company with the others.--They have been lodged in the Tower.

*The hostages at this time were Mouy, Palaiseau, La Ferté, and Nantouillet, provost of Paris, and their conduct had been so obnoxious they were retained for a while after the notification of peace on the surrender of Havre.

I wrote on the 19th instant saying that one of the hostages here from the king of France had refused to fly with the other three; but this was a mistake, as all four of them were taken together at Gravesend in a Flemish ship in which they had taken passage. It has been discovered that they took the step by orders of the Ambassador here at the command of their King. They are confined in the Tower of London, and are not allowed to communicate with anyone. The Ambassador says that by the terms of the treaty of Chateau Cambresi and in accordance with the protest made here in the King's name some months ago, the said hostages were quite justified in returning home the best way they could, and that it was not a breach of faith for them to do so.

They are busy here getting troops ready to send to Havre-de-Grâce in place of those that fall by pestilence. Not a day passes without 40 or more deaths. They are also trying to raise forces for the purpose of assaulting some place on the coast, and so diverting the King's troops and passing the summer in safety.

I am informed that the intention is to send this army to Calais as being the place most distant from the King's forces and the army that will be before Havre-de-Grâce, and also because they think that, having Flanders at their back, they will have less to guard against and an unlimited supply of provisions. They even assert that they will be joined there also by as many troops--horse and foot--as they require. I do not know whether they are mistaken in this or if indeed they do not publish it to arouse the suspicion of the French; but I know that they are declaring such to be case, and that the French ambassador has sent word of it to the King, not without apprehension that there may be some secret understanding between your Majesty and the Queen, and that men and supplies may mysteriously find their way from Flanders without orders from your Majesty.

Stukeley took leave of the Queen yesterday. He was to be accompanied by Jean Ribault and three other French pilots, who went on the same voyage last year sent by Admiral Chatillon. Ribault had promised to deliver to Stukeley a fort which he had built in that land and left garrisoned by 30 men. It appears, however, that Ribault repented of his promise to hand over to the English what French ships and money had gained, and determined to escape with the French hostages and was captured with them. The three pilots are still going, but Stukeley has put them in chains. Ribault is still a prisoner and they threaten to hang him. They say the Queen had given him 300 ducats of income and a house in return for the service he was to render in this discovery, and it is true that she offered him this, but he says that he had not accepted it.

ohn Hawkins is a captain who, I wrote to your Majesty, went to Guinea a little over a year ago, and arrived at Plymouth on the 25th ultimo. Having made his voyage to Guinea and taken slaves there, he sailed to the island of Santo Domingo, where they say by leave of the Governor he traded with the Spaniards, and brings over 50,000 ducats in gold and some pearls, hides, and sugar, as the payment for his slaves. On his return he touched at Florida, where he found some Frenchmen who bought a vessel of him and 20 barrels of flour to return to France. These Frenchmen were the rest of those who had gone there, as 70 of them who had gone to Cuba and Jamaica in search of provisions were all caught and hanged in Jamaica, so that not a single Frenchman remained in Florida. If Hawkins tells the truth about having permission from the Governor to trade freely in those islands, it would cause considerable inconvenience, unless measures be taken to prevent it in future, because the greed of these people is such that they might arrange to always undertake similar voyages, and besides usurping the trade of those who traffic under your Majesty's license, I do not believe that a ship would be safe if they were strong enough to take it. I will try to get information on this point and advise your Majesty.

I have been unable to learn anything fresh about Hawkins' voyage, except that he traded in Jamaica and Tierra Firme, with license of the Governors, which seems incredible to me. The truth cannot be concealed, as steps are being taken in various quarters to discover the real facts.

Stukeley, respecting whom your Majesty has been informed, has had an interview with me, and says he had an understanding with Bishop Quadra when he left here on his voyage to Florida, and that certain steps were taken at the time to advise your Majesty. He again gave me to understand the ardent desire he had to serve your Majesty, and he assured me the aim and object that these people had in sending the expedition was to build a fort there, so that if the land was rich and fertile they might have their foot in it to trade, and in the contrary case, to have a centre of operations to rob the other ships that go that way. The Spaniards here tell me that this man is a Catholic, and has always shown great desire to serve your Majesty. He is being detained here for certain goods taken from a Portuguese in a French vessel, which he brought out from Bayona in Galicia. So far as violating the port is concerned to capture an enemy's ship, that is not thought much of here in accordance with their laws. He says Sidney is very anxious to take him to Ireland in consequence of his great friendship with John O'Neil, by means of which he thinks for certain that, in case your Majesty were so pleased, he could effect something in that island. I did not reply to this, and he then asked me to think it over, as he wished to be of service to your Majesty, and had discussed the matter previously with Bishop Quadra. With regard to Florida, I quite believe that the French have been as anxious to obtain a footing there as these people, more for the purpose of being on the track of ships from New Spain and Peru than for any other reason, but what is expedient to be done is to get the trade away from them by every possible means in those parts, and to let no one pass without license from your Majesty under heavy penalties. This is easier said than done in so great a sea, but they say that if a good watch were kept at the island of Dominica much could be effected, as it is in the passage.

have tried to gain more particulars of the story that Stukeley had begun to tell me about Florida, and of which I advised your Majesty. He tells me that Ribaut, a French captain, being here in the year '63, the Queen summoned him (Stukeley) and told him that this Ribaut assured her that Florida was a very rich and important country, and since he had ships and means he could undertake the voyage thither, although she would not help him with money, or in any other way for the present, so that if your Majesty should complain she should be able to swear that the voyage had not been made by her orders. He was to have half of all he gained, which would be a very large sum, because even if the land were less rich than was said, it was still in the track of ships from New Spain and Peru and elsewhere, which surely he could take. He says he thereupon communicated with the bishop of Aquila, being a loyal servitor of your Majesty, and informed him of all that had passed, and they had agreed together that he should make his preparations for the voyage to prevent any other person from being ordered to undertake it, but when the ships were ready he was to bore some holes in them secretly, so that they might make water and gradually get rid of the men who were to ship on board of them, and so delay the enterprise until your Majesty were advised, with the determination of serving your Majesty with the said ships if you were pleased to accept him. He says the Bishop informed your Majesty of this, as he himself also did by means of a servant of the Bishop called Alejandro, but that he has never received an answer, although he is still willing to do as he says. They tell me he is a serviceable man and a Catholic, as he says he is. I have listened to him and thanked him for his goodwill.

He also spoke to me respecting Irish affairs concerning John O'Neil, to which I only replied by thanking him for his goodwill and closed the conversation. He said that even though at present I might not consider it a matter to be discussed, in a year's time or a little longer I should be glad to consider it. I made no reply as your Majesty has ordered me not to enter into this question.

Hawkins, who is the Captain, I advised your Majesty had recently arrived from the Indies, conversed with me the day before yesterday at the palace and said that he had been on a long voyage of which he was very tired, and had traded in various parts of the Indies with your Majesty's subjects, but with permission of the Governors, from whom he brings certificates to show that he has fulfilled the orders given to him by this Queen prior to his departure. I said that I should be glad for my own satisfaction and his to see the certificates, and he said he would show them to me. I asked him if it were true that all the Frenchmen who were in Florida had left, and he said they had, and that he had sold them a ship and victuals for their return, as I have already advised. He says the land is not worth much, and that the natives are savage and warlike.

I have not thought well to take any steps or make any representation about this voyage until I was well informed of the particulars. I am promised a detailed statement of the voyage--where he went and what he did, and, if possible, will enclose it herewith. The orders he received, however, according to the secret report of one of those who accompanied him, was to arrange with the natives and force them to trade with him, and that they out of fear, as he was well armed, agreed to trade, although they could easily have resisted him. The truth will be learnt.

have used all diligence to obtain information about *Hawkins' voyage, and find that after he left Galicia, where he touched, he went to Guinea, and traded with the Portuguese slavers. He obtained a number of Negroes and sent men on shore to obtain more. He took some, but lost nine soldiers killed, amongst whom were some Portuguese.*

They then touched at La Margarita, Carthagena, Cabo de la Vela, and other places, thus spending a fortnight awaiting the fleet from the mainland, or New Spain, in order if possible to capture one of the ships.

They intended to touch at Habana, but the weather was contrary, and they ran out by the Bahama channel and coasted along Florida, where they found the Frenchmen, to whom they gave 15 barrels of flour, and sold them a ship in which to return to France.

The man who gives me this account, and who went the whole voyage, tells me that Hawkins got a Spanish pilot out of a Portuguese ship, by whose aid the voyage was made, and who still remains secretly in the ship.

This Hawkins, as I wrote your Majesty, spoke to me in the palace, and I treated him courteously, although I had heard something of what I have mentioned, but wished to gain further particulars, and in order not to arouse his suspicions I asked him to dine with me, and he gave me a general account of the voyage, which corresponds with the information already given as regards the places he went to, but not as regards his mode of trading. On the contrary, he said he had traded greatly to the satisfaction of the Spaniards everywhere, and with license from the Governors, which he would show me. He told me, amongst other things, that he had a bill from one of the Governors for 600 dollars, which was to be paid to him in another island, where, however, he did not touch, on account of the bad weather. I asked whether it was true that he had found the Frenchmen in Florida and had sold them a ship and given them flour for the voyage home. He said yes, and that Pero

Melendez would find none of them there. He said that dissensions had broken out amongst them, and some of them had left their commander, most of whom had been captured in Jamaica, and about 20 had returned through stress of hunger to their captain in Florida, who hanged four of them whom he (Hawkins) had seen.

He told me that the land was not good nor the rivers either, and that he would not on any account undertake the voyage again.

The owners who provided the capital for him are, I am informed, dissatisfied with him, and believe he has brought more gold than he confesses. He on his part does not appear contented with the sum they have paid him and this may lead to the truth coming out. He is now rendering his accounts, and I learn from the person who has to receive them that he credits himself with 1,600 dollars given to one of the Governors for leave to trade, and also for the bill for 600 dollars from the other Governor which was not presented for payment in accordance with an arrangement between them, so that it might appear that the Governor had paid for what he had bought. This bill must be the one Hawkins told me he had from one of the Governors.

The voyage has brought him 60 per cent profit. They tell me that this profit has encouraged some of the merchants here to undertake other like voyages and even that Hawkins will return in May. This is important and needs decisive action. I could speak to the Queen and tell her that the man confesses to have traded in places where your Majesty has forbidden commerce, and request her to have him punished; but I want to have the matter very clear first.

our Majesty's letter the 2nd instant was received here on the 27th, with the statement as to the successful issue of Pero Melendez de Aviles' voyage to Florida. Thanks be to God, whose aid I pray may always cause your Majesty's affairs to prosper, since they all tend to His service.

On the 28th, I went to Greenwich, and after having saluted the Queen from your Majesty, told her of this voyage, and what had taken place previously with the King and Queen of France whose subjects had occupied Florida although it had already been taken possession of in your Majesty's name. I told her also the reply given by the French King, and that papers had been discovered, proving that the Admiral of France was the originator of the expedition, as also the instructions given by your Majesty to Don Francés de Alava, as to the communications to be addressed to the King and Queen of France.

The Queen seemed greatly pleased at the success of the voyage and asked me to thank your Majesty warmly for having informed her of it, as she was always pleased to receive good news from your Majesty. She marvelled greatly, however, that I should say that Florida had been discovered and taken possession of by your Majesty's subjects as she always understood that it had first been discovered by Captain Ribaut, who had come hither with the news of his discovery. She had indeed intended to send and conquer it. I told her it was notorious that it had been discovered as I said, and there was no room for doubt upon the subject.

She answered that if that were the case, she asked your Majesty's pardon for having thought of conquering it, and as regards the Admiral, she understood the French very well, but did not care to discuss their affairs, or to answer for them, as they were quite old enough to answer for themselves. I understood, however, from her words, that she disapproved of the Admiral's acts after the King and Queen had promised that their subjects should not go to your Majesty's dominions.

After leaving the Queen, I spoke with Cecil, and he said that he blamed the Admiral greatly, and the King of France ought to punish him severely. He said your Majesty should proclaim your rights with regard to Florida, that they might be known everywhere. I told him, as I had told the Queen, that the case was notorious, and that the French could not fail to have had full knowledge of it. After speaking to the Queen about Florida, she said she had received letters from Germany informing her of the troops your Majesty was raising there, and the preparations you were making to resist the Turks, and she had no doubt that they would be successful. She hoped as successful as in the Florida affair.

Captain Hawkins comes to ask me if I have any reply to his offers of service. I am told that certain persons wish to send with great secrecy two ships to the Indies, with merchandise, and to return with skins; but they are not quite decided. I am promised timely advice. There is great need to be on the alert everywhere to prevent these people from trading, or else to do them all possible harm, and so discourage them from going, because, beside the inadvisability of allowing them to trade, religion will suffer greatly.

Six or seven days ago an English sailor arrived here, who was on board a ship which Pero Melendez took from the English before the affair of Florida. He says that after Pero Melendez had defeated the French, as he wrote to your Majesty, they had returned, and the same wind had brought up Jean Ribaut with others to the same place Melendez had taken them, and had beheaded Ribaut. I thought this was another version of the events which Pero Melendez had described, but again questioned the sailor, and he assured me that this was not so, and that things had occurred as he related them, he himself having seen the execution of Ribault, whom he knew well.

I have some suspicion that Captain Hawkins wishes to make another voyage like the last, but I am not sufficiently sure to speak to the Queen about it. The French Ambassador here is leaving, his successor having arrived after having been expected for some time. I went to visit the new man and I found him with his predecessor and Mavissier. He said, amongst other things, that his King had grown greatly and was very lusty. I answered him that I was glad to hear this, but he had better not tell this Queen so or she would bring about the marriage at once. They all three looked at me and the late Ambassador said a word in French, as if in anger, signifying that everything was known. They have been negotiating secretly lately.

I went today to see Cecil who has been unwell, and in the course of conversation spoke of the Archduke's business, to which he appears very well disposed. I said to him "These "Frenchmen are in a fine taking when they see the Archduke's "match progressing, and at once bring their own King forward "to embarrass the Queen. When they see that this trick has "hindered the negotiation they take up with Leicester again and "think we do not see through them." He said they are so full of fine words and promises, to which I replied that they acted in the same way with everyone for their own ends. He said that they thought when they had Lord Robert on their side that their business was as good as done, and that he quite understood that the great object of the French was to embroil and incite enmity between the Emperor and your Majesty, and I think they must be doing the same thing here, although Cecil did not tell me so. He assured me, however, that they expressed great indignation at what had happened in Florida, and he said that at least they had no reason for any such feeling against your Majesty seeing the help you have given them in their necessity, although this Queen had not done so. I had a long conversation with him on these matters, and from what I could gather the French are again bringing up their King's marriage, and intend to proclaim that an injury has been done them in Florida. He remarked to me that he had news that the French were preparing another voyage thither, and I said it was hardly credible, but that if they went there again they would be punished as the others were.

From the Jeannette Thurber Connor manuscript collections in the Manuscript Division of the Library of Congress come the following essay and translations of three letters of Pedro Menéndez. Apparently Mrs. Connor had expected to publish these at a later date but never did so during her lifetime. As she points out, the letters give us an idea of the vigor and competence of the man.

Letters from Menéndez

OF THE FIFTY-NINE LETTERS of Pedro Menéndez in the second volume of Eugenio Ruidíaz y Caravia, *La Florida, su conquista y colonización por Pedro Menéndez de Avilés* (Madrid, 1893), most of which are addressed to King Philip II, the three presented here give a very comprehensive view of this many-sided genius. His brief, telegraphic style needs to be studied. Some sentences are not clear because his thoughts travel so quickly that his pen has not the time to shape them, and he omits countless details which are given by his biographers; but instead of these one finds plans of gigantic scope and rare far-sightedness, and enthusiasm for his task, which in his eyes had the dignity of a mission. The conquest, subjugation, and colonizing of Florida; the conversion of the Indians; the construction of forts for the security of the coast and the Bahama Channel; the exploration of the interior; the boundless possibilities of growing trade on the new continent; his constant need of money and reinforcements—these subjects fill more space in his letters than the fate of Fort Caroline and poor Ribault and his followers. Menéndez is always more discursive on what must be done than on what has been done; perhaps this is why, at the end of three and a half centuries, his personality stands out with such unusual distinctness. He does stop long enough, however, after mentioning Ribault's death, to give him such words of praise as Ribault himself might have liked to see on his tombstone; it was Ribault's greatest enemy who wrote his epitaph for history.

To Philip II[1]

The Adelantado Pero Menéndez. Eleventh of September, 1565. This is a duplicate of the other which has been received.

To the R.C.M. of the King Don Philip our lord, in his Royal Council.

R. C. M.[2]

 sailed from Puerto Rico on the fifteenth of August for Havana with the ships that I had with me, to join there the reinforcements from Santo Domingo, and proceed to these provinces of Florida; and I continued to prosecute my voyage, the appearance of the sun and moon seeming to me to indicate fair weather. I thought that, if I succeeded in arriving in those parts, at the harbor where the Frenchmen were, before the French fleet should arrive, I had sufficient force to take and hold it until the reinforcements from Santo Domingo and the troops that I needed should reach me, for the reason that the Frenchmen had built their fort five leagues up the river inland, and that there is a little island one league long at the mouth of the river,[3] within the harbor, which they must perforce pass along as they enter, and whoever should hold it, would be master of the sea; and it can easily be held, so that no ship can enter or go out of that harbor, without license from the Alcalde who may command there. Having learned this secret from three Frenchmen with me, whom Your Majesty ordered to be delivered to me, and who were the first who had been there; who also told me that, if the Frenchmen should arrive there before me, they would fortify this island so as to be masters of the sea and harbor; it seemed to me the best and most essential thing, as I found myself with eight hundred persons, five hundred of them soldiers who could be landed, and two hundred seamen, the other hundred being useless people, married men, women and children, and officials, to come to seek this port in order to take and fortify this little island. And having asked the advice thereon of the naval and military captains and officers, they were all of the same opinion, because it seemed to them that if we could arrive before the French fleet, the war would be at an end; and that when the horses from Santo Domingo should reach us, we should be masters of the campaign, both on land and on sea, and would keep them surrounded; and however strong they might be, we would be able to destroy them, without their being able to receive help, either by land or by sea. And so, being in accord, we pursued our straight course to these parts, and on the twenty-fifth of August, Sunday at noon, we discovered this land off Cape Canaveral, which is the latitude of 28 degrees, at the entrance of the Bahama Channel, and we sailed along the coast, seeking that harbor, as far as 29 degrees, for such was the report that I had, that the Frenchmen were between 28 and 29 degrees. Not finding them, we went on as far as 29.5 degrees; and having seen fires on the shore on the second of September, I ordered a captain ashore with twenty soldiers, to try to get an interpreter among the Indians, that they might give us knowledge of that harbor; and so the captain who went ashore joined them and talked to them, and they told him, by signs, that the harbor was further on, in a higher latitude towards the north; and they having returned the same day with this answer, I determined the next day in the morning to go ashore myself to see these Indians, who seemed to me to be a noble race, and I took some things as gifts for them. They were well pleased with me, assuring me that the harbor was further on; and so we went on our way to seek it, and I sailed thence in search of it on the fourth of September; and the same day, at two in the afternoon, we discovered it, and four vessels anchored off there, showing the standards of the flagship and the Admiral's ship. Being certain that the succor had come to them, and that by falling suddenly on these four vessels we should be able to take them, I decided to go and attack them; and being at half a league from them, there came up great thunder and lightning and rain, and then the wind left us becalmed; but about ten at night it came on to blow again, and as it appeared to me that, in the morning, the ships that might be in the harbor would come out with reinforcements for these four, I resolved to go and anchor alongside thereof, in order to attack them at daybreak, and so I did; for I anchored between the flagship and the Admiral's with my flagship; and having spoken to them, asking what they were doing there, and what captain they had, they answered that they had Jean Ribault for Captain-General, and that they had come to this country by command of the King of France; and they asked what ships ours were, and what General we carried.

They were answered that he was Pedro Menéndez, who by order of Your Majesty had come to this coast and land to burn and hang the French Lutherans that might be found there, and that in the morning he would board their vessels to see if they were that people, for if they were he could not fail to execute upon them the justice that Your Majesty commanded. They answered that that was not good, and that I could come on at once without waiting until morning; and as it appeared to me that this opportunity was not to be lost, although it was night, the poop of my ship being at their prow, I ordered cable to be paid out, so as to come alongside of her, but they cut their cables, and hoisted their sails, and all four of them took to flight. We were able to fire five heavy guns at their Admiral's ship, and we suspected that we sank her, for many people abandoned her, and got into a large boat of twenty oars, in the form of a pinnace; and going between the vessels, they put themselves aboard another ship, leaving the boat. I chased the three ships that night, but as my galleon was dismasted by the storm, they sailed faster than I; and so, at dawn, finding them five or six leagues distant, I returned to the harbor to land five hundred soldiers on the little island; and being yet half a league therefrom, we perceived three ships anchored close to it with many flags and pennants flying, and on shore two field banners; and as it appeared

to me that there was no reason for wasting time there, since this flagship I have brought could not go in, and the small ships could enter only with great risk, I decided to turn back toward the Bahama Channel to seek a harbor where I could land near them; and at eight leagues from their harbor by sea, and six by land, I found one which I had reconnoitered before, on St. Augustine's Day, being in barely 30.5 degrees. There, on the sixth of this month, I landed two hundred soldiers; and on the seventh, three small vessels went in with another three hundred, and the married men with their wives and children; and I unloaded most of the artillery and munitions I was carrying; and on the eighth, being Our Lady's Day, while we were landing another hundred persons who were to go on shore, with some artillery and ammunition, and many supplies, the flagship and Admiral's ship of the French came down within a half league of us, offering us battle, sailing round and round us; and we, anchored as we were, made signs to them to board us. At three in the afternoon, they hoisted sails and went to their harbor; and I went ashore and took possession in the name of Your Majesty and was sworn in by the captains and officers, as Governor and Captain-General and Adelantado of this land and coast, in accordance with Your Majesty's instructions.

Many Indians were present, and many chiefs were among

150

them. They show themselves to be our friends, and appear to us to be enemies of the French. They told us that inside this harbor, and without going out to sea, we can come to the Frenchmen's river in front of the fort, by going up the river seven or eight leagues; which is a very good thing, on account of being able to carry up the artillery and camp stores and horses if we should wish to land near their fort, without our being hindered by their island, even though they have fortified it; especially as we can go by land with horses and artillery. I decided to fortify myself as well as I can until succor shall come, and within three days I shall send to Havana on a short voyage, for with God's help I hope they will make the journey within eight or ten days, and I shall send pilots so that the succor can come with all dispatch to this port; for when it arrives I shall so exert myself, with the help of Our Lord, that I shall take from them the island of that harbor, and plant the artillery upon their fort; for with the horses I hope in God to do so with safety, and be master of the country. The Indians of this harbor tell us that ten ships have come to them in these parts in the last month, and that many caciques are friendly to them; and so we hold it for certain that they will come upon us with the Indians who are their friends, and likewise upon this galleon; and as she is loaded with such a quantity of stores, artillery and ammunition, it would be our total destruction if they should take her from us; and if they attack her, having but a small crew, she will be in danger, as I have been sailing her for fifteen days along this coast, among many sandbanks and currents, so as to get near the harbors to reconnoiter them, and to unload what I have unloaded. She is near the coast, and if any side winds or bad weather should come, she will be lost. We need at least another fifteen days to finish unloading and to take in ballast, and in this time it would be a miracle, in case of a storm or attack from the enemy, if she could escape with all she contains; and so I have finished landing all the artillery and ammunition that was on board of her, and I am sending her to Hispaniola or Monte Cristo or Puerto Real, that she may be laid up there, with a quantity of biscuit and some wine which I cannot unload. I shall send there for these provisions in the coming month of January, as we have biscuit on hand for the whole month of December; and with the good regulations we shall have, we will make it last through the whole of January; and if it be advisable that at the beginning of summer this galleon should come out armed to this coast she will be mistress of the sea, while in the meantime I make myself stronger on land so as to intercept the supplies that may come to the French; that is, if the Audiencia of Santo Domingo will pay the amount due for equipment, and pay the crew, and provision her, for without this she cannot sail, as there will be no possibility of paying.

It appears to me that what I shall have most need of will be horses, for of those that sailed from Puerto Rico, only one arrived alive, and it is fitting that every soldier should be mounted, to become master of the country, and to prevent the Indians from having relations with the Frenchmen, and the Frenchmen from setting out from their fort; for when the Indians see this, and that the Frenchmen fear us, and that we are stronger than they, they will all be our friends; and this I shall endeavor to bring about with all possible diligence, on account of the great importance of gaining reputation with them, and of their fearing us; while, in order that they may love us, I shall make them all the presents possible. I find myself with two shallops of between seventy and eighty toneles each, very good vessels, drawing very little water, and I am sending them to Havana, for each will bring back eleven horses, if orders have been given there to this effect. It would be a great thing, and I am writing about it to the Governor and am sending him a note of hand so that Your Majesty may order it paid to me, as I shall pay for them; and when the vessels have come back with the horses (or if they come without them), I shall send them at once to Puerto de Plata, or Monte Cristo, to load horses, and shall write to the Audiencia of Santo Domingo to pay for them and hold them in readiness; and if they will not, I will send them a note of hand to pay for them; because the chief cost of the horses will be for the vessels and crews, for, as each vessel can carry forty horses, they will cost, one with another, one thousand ducats; for they must be good field horses, large-boned and able to work; likewise for herdsmen; and a vessel that should bring them--with the carpenter work done, the crews and salaries and supplies paid; the ship fitted out and armed; careened, and made ready for this coast as she should be, with cables, double anchors and tackle--each bark must cost at least two thousand ducats. As for me, Your Majesty can be certain that if I had a million more or less, I would lay out and expend the whole of it in this enterprise, which is so much for the service of God Our Lord, for the increase of our Holy Catholic Faith, and for the service of Your Majesty. And so have I offered to Our Lord all that he may give me in this world; all that I may possess, earn or acquire, in order to implant the Gospel in this land and enlighten the natives thereof, and so do I promise Your Majesty.

It will be well that Your Majesty should write immediately to the Governor of Puerto Rico, the Audiencia of Santo Domingo, and the Govenor of Havana, that every time my ships shall come into port there, they shall give them all aid and favor, and the horses that I may send to ask for, with food and water alone, and nothing else; and that there be no horse that will cost less than twenty-five or thirty ducats, and that these be the best for the price that there are in the land. As to the saddles and bridles, which must cost more, I do not wish them to furnish them, for I will send to Spain for them; and in this manner, even if it be at the cost of my whole substance, I shall soon have a supply of horses in these parts; and Your Majesty will be pleased to do me the favor to command that I shall be paid for this expense I am incurring in things which may be required, and Your Majesty should be pleased to do so. And inasmuch as I shall write to Your Majesty in a few days, I have no more to say for the present in this letter, except that the people who have come with me are working with great zeal and good will, so that it appears that Our Lord visibly strengthens and encourages them therefor, whereat I feel the greatest joy.

With the first two hundred soldiers I sent on shore two captains, who were Juan de San Vicente, a brother of Captain San Vicente, and Andrés López Patiño, both veteran soldiers, in order that they might throw up a trench in the most suitable place in which they could fortify themselves and gather together the people that were landed, so as to defend them from enemies if any should come upon them; and they did this so well that when I landed on Our Lady's Day, to take possession of the country in Your Majesty's name, it seemed as if they had had a month's time; and if they had had shovels, pickaxes, and other iron tools, they could not have done it better; although we have none of these things, because the ship which is bringing them has not arrived; but I have smiths and iron so that I can have them made with dispatch, and this I shall do. When I go on shore, we shall reconnoiter the places that appear to us most suitable in which to fortify ourselves, because the place where we now are is not so; and this we must do with the greatest speed, before the enemy can attack us; and if they give us eight days more time, we think we shall do it. I have appointed as my lieutenant and camp master, Pedro Menéndez de Valdés, to whom I have agreed to marry my daughter, and on whom Your Majesty was pleased to confer the Order of Santiago, who embarked secretly and against my will at Cádiz. He has been a soldier in Italy, of five or six years' service, reared in the galleys, and is a man of sense and of good understanding, with whom the men are well pleased. I have appointed as sergeant major Gonzalo de Villarroel, a good soldier, of good family, who has sense; I have appointed ten captains, all men of good family and trustworthy, and most of them men of experience; and to those who have not so much experience, though they be few, I have given soldiers of

Italy skilled in war for sergeants and ensigns; and each company is of fifty soldiers, and no more. When more troops arrive, I shall re-form these companies of infantry and cavalry, as it is expedient that there should be few men in each company, so as to have good discipline among the soldiers, and that they may be well drilled in arms in a short time; likewise that the Indians may be very well treated, and that the captains shall arm themselves with the strong armor of patience to endure labors, and be obedient to their General; and as to him who shall not do this, and who shall be known to make no efforts therefor, I shall take away his office, but shall not, for that reason, cease to honor him; and so, not being adapted to these labors, he can then eat and stretch out his legs and sleep at his ease; and in this manner I think I shall manage during the time I may be in these parts. The captains appointed are the following: Bartolomé Menéndez, my brother, one of Your Majesty's regular naval captains; Juan de San Vicente, Andrés López Patiño, Diego Alvarado, Alonso de Medrano, Francisco de Recalde, Martín Ochoa, Pedro de la Randia, Diego de Amaya, Francisco de Moxica. Diego Flórez de Valdés I have brought as Admiral of this fleet, and I shall send him to Havana within three days, with the two shallops, so that he may bring back the fleet that is there; and when he returns, if he brings the ships from the Asturias, I shall have a reasonable supply of seamen, especially as among them will be Diego Florez de Valdés, Estevan de las Alas, and Pedro Menéndez Marqués, my nephew, either one of whom is able to command the fleet; while in my company I have Diego de Amaya, to whom I have given a company of infantry, for he is a skillful man, a general in all things and a great seaman. I brought him out from Spain as head pilot, and he has done very well. I shall always take him with me in the field with his company, for the crossing of the arms of rivers and the navigation of the brigantines and boats that we must have in order to navigate the river, and take our artillery over, wherein he will aid me greatly. There are also among these people, and those who are to come from Biscay, many gentlemen who have not seen service, and others who are good soldiers, who come with great zeal and love to serve Your Majesty. It would be well if Your Majesty would write, thanking them for undertaking the voyage and promising them every favor and reward, for this will animate them to endure with the more zeal all sorts of toils and dangers; and as this country is very large, it will be best, in time, to portion it out among those who may deserve it, to the end that they may bring out here their kindred and relatives, and that the Gospel may be established with more of a foundation of men of noble birth.

It will be well that Your Majesty shall order that, with every horse that I shall ship for these provinces, they send me a supply of maize for the first year, for although the whole supply cannot come with the horses, I shall send for it every four months; and for the future, after this year, I shall give orders for the planting of grain and maize, in order that they shall have something to eat here, for in no manner is it proper to take it from the Indians, so that they shall not take up enmity against us; rather will it be proper for us to give food to those who have it not, so that they shall have love and firm friendship for us.

Seven or eight leagues from this place, where I went on shore on the second of September, to speak with those Indians who gave us information that the harbor of the French was farther north, we found great signs of gold, both ordinary and fine, which the Indians had on them, suspended from their ears and lips and on their arms. I did not allow any to be taken from them, that they should not suppose that we were covetous of it, although they did give one soldier a small piece of more than twenty-two carats.

May our Lord protect and increase the Royal Catholic Person of Your Majesty, with an increase of greater kingdoms and dominions, as Christendom has need thereof and we Your Majesty's servants desire. From these provinces of Florida, on the eleventh of September in the year 1565.

Your Majesty's humble servant, who kisses your Royal hands.

P. Menéndez

NOTES

1. Archivo General de Indias, Seville, estante 54-cajón 5-legajo 16. This letter was translated from a copy (Connor Papers, Library of Congress) of the original in Seville. Other copies are in the Colección Navarrete at the Depósito Hidrográfico, Madrid; the Woodbury Lowery Collection in the Library of Congress; the Buckingham Smith Collection at the New York Historical Society; and at the Massachusetts Historical Society. It is published in Eugenio Ruidíaz y Caravia, *La Florida: su conquista y colonización por Pedro Menéndez de Avilés* (2 vols.; Madrid, 1893), II, 74-84; a translation is in the *Proceedings of the Massachusetts Historical Society*, 2d Series, VIII, 419-25.

In this letter Menéndez tells of his fight with Ribault's French ships, which he puts to flight. He lands at the port which is now St. Augustine and takes possession of it as Adelantado and Captain-General of Florida. He emphasizes his need of horses, going into details as to their price and quality; speaks of nominations of officials made by him; and gives advice as to the rewards which should be given them.

2. R.C.M. signifies Royal Catholic Majesty; it is C.R.M. in Spanish, Católica Real Majestad.

3. Fort George Island. Its Indian name was Alimacani.

To a Jesuit Friend[1]

hrough letters from Pedro del Castillo I have heard of the many favors done me in all those kingdoms, by the Order of the Society of Jesus: and by means of their prayers, Our Lord has granted me many mercies, and does each day, giving me victory and success in all the things to which we have set our hand, I and the Spaniards who are with me, since we arrived in these provinces. And although we have suffered the greatest hunger, hardships, and perils, and there have been some who could not endure them, and who, like weak men, became discouraged; yet others never felt them, and I among them, although the greatest sinner of them all, for I was certain I was undergoing them for Our Lord, and his reward would not fail me; and I went about more hale and hearty, contented, and cheerful than ever I had been, even in the period of greatest need, when each week the Indians came two or three times, killing two or three of our men and wounding others, and we had nothing to eat; nor had those of us in one fort known for two months whether those in the other were dead or alive. On the eve of St. Peter's Day, (on that same day I sailed from Spain with the Armada, bound for this land), seventeen ships appeared off this harbor of St. Augustine, and all entered safely.[2] They brought fifteen hundred soldiers and five hundred sailors, much artillery and munitions, and were all laden with supplies; whereupon everyone received great pleasure and consolation, and those who were in this fort would meet one another, weeping for joy, their eyes and hands raised to heaven, praising Our Lord.

At that time I was not in this fort. I came within eight days: and when I did, I saw all the goods and succor that His Majesty the King Don Philip was sending us, and that Our Lord had brought them in safety.

On the one hand, I received the greatest satisfaction at seeing how well the King our Lord had aided us; but on the other, I felt distressed and lost, on seeing that no one from the Society had come, nor indeed any learned religious;[3] for on account of the many caciques we have for friends, the good judgment

156

and understanding of the natives of these provinces, and the great desire they have to become Christians and know the Law of Jesus Christ, six such religious could accomplish more in one month than many thousands of men such as we could in many years; we even need them for our own instruction. And it is wasted time to think that the Holy Gospel can be established in this land with the army alone. Your worship may be certain, if I am not mistaken, that the Word of Our Lord will spread in these parts; for the ceremonies of these people consist in great measure in adoring the sun and moon, and dead deer and other animals they hold as idols; and each year they have three or four festivals for their devotions, during which they worship the sun, and remain three days without eating, drinking, or sleeping; these are their fast days. And he who is weak, and cannot endure this, is considered a bad Indian, and therefore looked upon with contempt by their noble caste; and he who comes through these hardships the best is held to be one of the most important men, and treated with utmost courtesy.

They are a people of much strength; very agile and swift, and great swimmers; they carry on many wars against one another, and no powerful cacique is known among them.[4] I have not wanted to be friends with any cacique in order to make war on his enemy, even though he were also mine, because I tell

them that Our Lord is in heaven, and is the Cacique of all the caciques of the earth, and of all that which is created; and He is angry with them because they make war and kill one another like beasts. And thus a few have allowed me to make them friends, and have left their idols and asked me to give them crosses before which they may worship; I have already given them some, and they worship them, and I have given them some youths and soldiers to teach them the Christian Doctrine.

They have begged me to let them become Christians like us, and I have replied to them that I am expecting your worships, in order that you may make vocabularies and soon learn their language; and that then you will tell them how to become Christians, and undeceive them as to how, not being so, they serve and hold for their Master the most wicked creature in the world, who is the devil, and that he misleads them; but once they are Christians, they will be undeceived and serve Our Lord, who is the Cacique of heaven and earth; and then, happy and joyful, they will be our brothers in truth and we will give them of what we may have.

And as I had told them that with this expected succor, these religious would come, who would soon be able to talk to them and teach them to be Christians; and they did not come-- the Indians held me to be a liar, and some of them have become irritated, saying that I am deceiving them; and the caciques, my enemies, laugh at them and at me.

It has done the greatest harm, that none of your worships, nor any other learned religious, have come to instruct these people; for as they are great traitors and liars, if, with time and labor, peace with them is not confirmed, so as to open the door to the preaching of the Holy Gospel, the caciques confirming what the religious say, later we shall accomplish nothing, they thinking that we deceive them. May Our Lord inspire that good Society of Jesus to send to these parts as many as six of its members--may they be such--for they will certainly reap the greatest reward.

On the fourteenth of September, 1566, with a contrary wind, there arrived a vessel near this harbor of St. Augustine, about two leagues therefrom; and as it appeared to me that she did not recognize the harbor, I sent a boat, equipped as a skiff with many oars, to get her inside; but there was a heavy sea, and the tide was contrary, and the boat could not go out, and within two days a tempest arose.[5] Fifteen days afterwards a boat was found, anchored, with six Flemings aboard, and no supplies of any kind, in the river of Fort San Mateo, near the sea; and two of the men were wounded to death with arrows. There was likewise a Spaniard among them.

They said that the day before, one league from there, Indians, our enemies, had killed Father Martínez, of the Society, and three other men; and that the ship which had passed by here was the hooker on board in which he came, and she did not recognize the harbor; and it was fifteen days since the pilot of the hooker had landed them in the boat, to try to reconnoiter where they were; and as a storm came up, they could not return to the hooker; and that all these days they had met with many Indians who said they were my friends and brothers; that they had received and entertained them very well, and one league from the Fort of San Mateo this misfortune had happened to them; that Father Martínez brought all the messages from the Holy Father, and these and all the rest he brought were lost. Blessed be Our Lord in all things. And since the Divine Majesty permits and wills it so to be, let us give infinite thanks for it all: since those of us who are here deserve so little that Our Lord desired to give us this calamity by removing from our company such a blessing as was Father Martínez, of whom we Spaniards who are in this land, stood in such need, as well as the natives thereof.[6]

I have believed that the hooker has not been lost, and that she has arrived at the island of Puerto Rico, or Santo Domingo, or Cuba. I am dispatching a boat to go to these islands and aboard her a servant of mine; and wherever that hooker may wish to go, I have ordered her pilot to sail to Havana; and he is to carry with him and take care of the two Fathers of the Society who are coming on her; and they shall busy themselves until the end of February, when the winter shall be passed, in preparing vocabularies and learning the language of the land of Carlos, a cacique who is a great friend. And there in Havana there are people who know the language very well; and at the beginning of March they shall go in two days to that cacique, for the sailing is very good; and then to these forts, without again embarking, and through a land which is thickly settled; for most of the villages through which they have to pass are our friends; they have crosses that I have given them, and youths and soldiers who are teaching them the doctrine.

We have not gone inland, because of fortifying ourselves on the coast and trying to make friends with its caciques, so that we can feel secure behind our backs; and therefore we have not seen any large towns, although there are many Indians and boys. There is news that inland there are many people, and a great report of a Salt River which goes to China; wherefore it is expedient that the religious who may come to these parts be truly religious; otherwise, it were better that they should not come. And since your worship understands this better than I can write

it, this is enough so that the Society may provide what is fitting in the matter.

I shall be in those kingdoms some time in May, at the latest; and, it may be, many days before; and it would not suit me to remain in those kingdoms later than July, that I may return to this coast in good weather, and bring over in the greatest safety the persons who may come with me, because then the weather and the navigation are good for coming to these provinces.

And I shall bring and serve and entertain those members of the Society, and any other religious who may wish to come, as if they were the King himself; and I shall give orders in these parts, as long as I live, that they be respected as Our Lord's Ministers, trusting that he who may not deserve this treatment shall be brought to deserve it by his companions; and in case they were unable to do this, they should send him back to those kingdoms; because in this new land it is needful that all this should be. And it is a thing with which God Our Lord will be most pleased because it is from the religious that all good teaching and example must come, and for this reason he must be respected and revered.

Many times I kiss the hands of all those gentlemen of the Society; may they have the reward of Our Lord for the many favors they do me in entreating Our Lord to help and protect *me in all things. And I therefore beg them as a mercy, as much as I can, to continue to do so. And if this should reach your worship in Cadiz, tell Pedro del Castillo that I kiss his hands, and he is to consider this letter as his.*

May Our Lord keep and increase your worship's most magnificent person and estate, as I desire. From Florida, from this Fort of St. Augustine, on the fifteenth of October, of the year 1566.

Your worship's servant,

Pero Menéndez

NOTES

1. Published in Ruidíaz, *La Florida,* II, 154-60; and in Father Alcázar, *Historia de la Compañía de Jesús en la provincia de Toledo,* II, 153. A translation is in the *Historical Magazine* (October, 1861), 292-94. If the original is in the archives at either Seville or Simancas, it has not yet been found.

In this letter Menéndez speaks of the arrival of Sancho de Arciniega and his fleet; of the character of the Indians; of the need for more priest-teachers to work with the Indians; and of the murder (September 28, 1566) by the Indians of the Jesuit Father Pedro Martínez.

2. Sancho de Arciniega and his fleet.

3. The adjectival noun "religious" signifies the priests of a religious order (Jesuits, Franciscans, etc.); Menéndez is here pleading for priests of the Society of Jesus to be sent to convert and teach the Indians (C.E.B.).

4. What about Saturiba, Outina, and Carlos, among others?

5. A year previous, at that season, Ribault's ships had been wrecked in such a storm.

6. An original account of this episode, written by Father Juan Rogel who came with Father Martínez, his superior, but remained aboard the ship, is in Felix Zubillaga, S.J. (ed.), *Monumenta antiquae Floridae, 1566-1572* (Rome, 1946), pp. 101-28 (C.E.B.).

7. " . . . por tener las espaldas seguras."

To Philip II[1]

I wrote to your Majesty by the galleon *San Salvador* on the tenth of September, the day on which she left from this port; the duplicate of the letter goes with this one; and immediately after, within that very hour, I being on the bar in a shallop, with two boats laden with artillery and munitions, the four French galleons we had pursued came upon us, with two other pinnaces at the poop, to prevent our disembarking here, and to take from us our artillery and supplies; and although the time was unfavorable for crossing the bar, I preferred to fight, at the risk of drowning myself there with one hundred and fifty persons who were with me, and with the bronze artillery and demi-culverins, rather than see myself in their power and thus strengthen them. It was Our Lord's will to save us miraculously, for the tide was low and there was but a scant fathom and a half of water on the bar, while the ship needed a full fathom and a half; and they, seeing I had escaped them, came to talk with me, saying I should surrender and have no fear, and then went off to search for the galleon, for let it be understood that they held she could not escape from them. Within two days a hurricane and very great storm came upon them, and as it seemed to me that they could not have returned to their fort, that they were in danger of shipwreck, and that to come to look for me as they had, they must have brought with them the greater part of the best forces they had; that their fort would remain weakened, and that now was the opportunity to go and attack it. I discussed with the captains the fine undertaking we might carry through, and it appeared so to them likewise; I at once had five hundred men equipped--three hundred arquebusiers, the others with pikes and bucklers, although there were few of these last--and we made up our knapsacks, wherein each man put six pounds of biscuit which he carried on his back; also his wine bottle, containing from three quarts to a gallon of wine,[2] and his arms; for each captain and soldier, and I first to set the example, carried this food and the arms on his back. As we did not know the way, we thought we should arrive in two days, and that there would be but six or eight leagues to march, for so two Indians who came with us had told us by signs. Setting out from this Fort of St. Augustine in this order and with this determination, on the eighteenth of September we met with rivers so swollen by the great rainfall, that by the evening of the nineteenth we had walked at least fifteen leagues, when we encamped one league from the fort more or less; more than fifteen leagues, in order to avoid the rivers, all through swamps and wilderness, through a region never before trod. On the twentieth, the eve of the day of the blessed apostle and evangelist *San Mateo*, at dawn when the day was breaking, we prayed to Our Lord and His Blessed Mother, beseeching them to give us victory over those Lutherans, as we had already agreed to attack openly with twenty ladders which we were carrying; and His Divine Majesty granted us such favor, and guided events in such a manner, that we took the fortress and all that it contained without the slaughter of a single man of ours, and with the wounding of but one, who has already recovered. One hundred and thirty-two men were killed, and next day ten more, who were captured in the woods, and among them many gentlemen; and he who was governor and alcalde, who called himself *Monsieur Laudonnière*, a relative of the Admiral of France, and who had been his major-domo, fled to the woods; a soldier pursued him and dealt him

a blow with his pike; we can not find out what has become of him. About fifty or sixty persons escaped either to the woods, or by swimming, or in two boats of the three ships which they had in front of the fort. I sent at once to their ships a trumpeter to make them surrender, and give up their arms and vessels, but they would not. We sent one of the ships to the bottom with artillery which was there in the fort, and the other [3] rescued the people and went down stream, where one league away, there were two other ships with many supplies, which were among the seven that had come from France, and had not yet been unloaded.

As it appeared to me that I ought not to lose this prize, I set out for this Fort of *Saint Augustine* to prepare three boats that were here, with which to go in search of them, but they were warned by the Indians; and since the French were few in number, they took the two best ships of the three they had, and sank the other; within three days they fled, and being advised of this, I gave up my journey. My men wrote me from the fort that after those ships had departed, there appeared in the woods about twenty Frenchmen, who go about in their shirts, many of them wounded, and it is thought that among them may be *Monsieur Laudonnière*. I have dispatched orders that they shall try to capture them by every means possible, and work justice upon them. There were found, counting women, girls, and boys under fifteen years, about fifty persons, and very great is my anxiety at seeing them in the company of my people, because of their evil sect, and I feared Our Lord would punish me if I used cruelty towards them, for eight or ten of the boys were born here. These Frenchmen had many friends among the Indians, who have shown much sorrow for their loss, especially for that of two or three teachers of their wicked doctrine who taught the caciques and Indians, who followed around after them as the apostles followed Our Lord, for it is a marvelous thing to see how the Lutherans have bewitched this poor savage people. I shall try everything possible to gain the good will of these Indians who were friends of these Frenchmen, and to have no occasion to break with them; for if one does not resist them by action, they are such great traitors and thieves and so envious, that one cannot well live with them. The caciques and Indians who are their enemies all show me friendship, which I keep and shall keep with them, even if it be not to their liking, for their malicious disposition shall play no part in making me do anything else.

On the twenty-eighth of September the Indians came to inform me that many Frenchmen were six leagues from here by the seashore, who had lost their ships, and had escaped by swimming and in the boats. I took fifty soldiers and arrived with them at break of day; and keeping my people in ambush, I went forth with one companion along a river, as they were on the other side and I on this. I spoke with them and told them I was Spanish, and they told me they were French; they asked me, either with or without my companion, to swim the river to where they were, as it was narrow. I replied that we did not know how to swim; that one of them should cross over, upon assurance of safety. They agreed to do it, and sent over a man of good understanding, a shipmaster.

He related to me in detail that they had sailed from their fort with four galleons and eight pinnaces which each carried twenty-four oars, with four hundred picked soldiers and two hundred sailors; Juan Ribao (Jean Ribault) as General, Monsieur La Grange who was General of the infantry, and other good captains and soldiers and gentlemen, with the intention of seeking and engaging me at sea; and, in case I had landed, of landing their forces in those pinnaces and attacking me. He said that if they had wished to land, they could well have done so, but they had not dared; and that desiring to return to their fort, a hurricane and storm overtook them, so that from twenty to twenty-five leagues from here three of their galleons were destroyed; and they carried about four hundred persons, of whom one hundred and forty only were there alive; as to the rest, some had been drowned, others killed by the Indians, and about fifty of them the Indians had captured and carried away; that Jean Ribault with his flagship was five leagues from them, anchored in three fathoms, aground on some shoals, without any masts, for he had had them cut down, and that there were on board the ship about two hundred people, little less; that they believe he is lost; and that all the bronze artillery, whereof there were many and very good pieces, with the ammunition, were lost in those three vessels; that part of them were on the ship of Jean Ribault, and they considered that he was certainly lost. And he told me that his companions, those captains and soldiers who were safe, prayed that I should give them safe conduct to go to their fort, since they were not at war with Spaniards. I answered him that we had taken their fort and killed those in it, because they had erected it there without Your Majesty's permission, and because they were implanting their evil Lutheran sect in these Your Majesty's provinces; and that I, as Governor and Captain-General of these provinces, would wage a war of fire and blood against all those who should come to people these lands and implant the wicked Lutheran sect; seeing that I had come by Your Majesty's command to spread the Gospel in these parts, to enlighten the natives as to what the Holy Mother Church of Rome says and believes, so that they may save their souls; and that therefore I would not give them safe conduct; rather would I follow them on land and sea, until I had taken their lives. He begged me to let him return with this message, and he promised that he would swim back at night; he asked also that I should grant him his life. I did it because I saw he was dealing truthfully with me, and he could make clear to me many things; and immediately after he had returned to his companions, there came a gentleman to tempt me, Monsieur Laudonnière's lieutenant, who was very crafty in these matters; and having conferred with me, he offered that they should lay down their arms, and give themselves up, provided I spared their lives. I replied to him that they could give up their arms, and place themselves at my mercy, for me to do with them that which Our Lord should command me; and from this he could not move me, nor will he, unless God Our Lord inspire me otherwise. And thus he went back with this answer, and they came over and laid down their arms, and I had their hands tied behind them, and had them put to the knife.[4]

Only sixteen were left,[5] of whom twelve were Breton sailors whom they had kidnapped, the other four being carpenters and calkers, people of whom I had need. It appeared to me that to chastise them in this manner would be serving God Our Lord and Your Majesty, so that henceforth this wicked sect shall leave us more free to implant the Gospel in these parts, enlighten the natives, and bring them to allegiance to Your Majesty; and forasmuch as this land is very large, there will be much to do these fifty years, but good beginnings give hope of good endings, and so I hope in Our Lord that He will give me success in everything, that I and my descendants may give these kingdoms to Your Majesty free and un-obstructed, and that the people thereof may become Christians; for this is what particularly interests me, as I have written to Your Majesty; and we shall gain much reputation with the Indians, and shall be feared by them, even though we make them gifts.

Meditating on what Jean Ribault had done, I concluded that within ten leagues of where he was anchored with his ship, the three other ships of his company had been lost; that whether he should be wrecked or whether he abandoned his ship, he would land his forces and entrench himself, landing what provisions he could from his ship, and would occupy himself in getting out what bronze guns he could from the three ships; that if his vessel were not lost he would repair damages as best he could from the masts and rigging of the other three ships, and would come back to the fort, thinking it still his; but that if the ship were lost, getting together all the forces he could, he would march along the shore. If he does this, I am waiting for him, so that, with God's help, he will be destroyed; yet he may go inland to a cacique who is friendly to him and very powerful, who is about thirty leagues distant from him; and if this is the case I shall go there to seek him, for it is not fitting that he or his companions remain alive; and if he comes with his ship to the fort, I have provided[6] at the bar two cannon and two demi-culverins wherewith to send him to the bottom after he shall have entered; a brigantine is kept in readiness to capture the men, and I shall do everything possible to prevent him from escaping.

The articles found in the fort were only four bronze pieces, of from ten to fifteen quintals, because as they had brought their cannons from France dismounted and as ballast, they took all the others, and all the rest of the munitions, on the galleons when they went in search of me. There were found, besides, twenty-five bronze muskets weighing two quintals; about twenty quintals of powder, and all the ammunition for these pieces; one hundred and seventy casks of flour, three to a ton; about twenty pipes of wine, as they had not unloaded the greater part of the supplies. For they were in doubt as to fortifying them-selves in that harbor, for fear that I might come and disembark there. They might have done so, but since they had come they had wasted their days in revelry, rejoicing in their arrival, be-cause they had heard the news that one hundred leagues north-northwest of Santa Elena, they hold the mountain ridge that comes from Zacatecas[7] and that there is much silver there. Indians had come to them with many pieces thereof, and the Indians of those parts had brought them a quantity worth five or six thousand ducats. There was found a quantity worth three thousand ducats, more or less, of cloth materials and all kinds of articles for barter; some hogs, male and female, and likewise some sheep and asses; all this the soldiers sacked without a thing escaping, except the artillery, ammunition, and flour.

There were likewise in the harbor, besides the two vessels there and the two near the bar, two others which they had stolen near Yaguana, laden with hides and sugar; the crews they had thrown overboard, and the cargo they had given to some English ships, to sell in France or England; two prominent Englishmen had remained as hostages, as the French had no sailors to take the ships across. These two Englishmen were killed when the fort was captured. The Englishmen to whom the cargo was entrusted had put into the harbor where the Frenchmen were, at the beginning of August of this year. That harbor is near the place where they had the fort which we took from them. The English vessel was a galleon of one thousand tons belonging to the Queen of England, with three tiers of very heavy artillery, and it is certain, say those that saw her, that never has a ship so well armed been seen, and she drew very little water. The three other vessels were smaller. It was agreed between these Englishmen and Frenchmen that since the French expected succor from France, Monsieur Laudonnière, who was Governor here, should go to France to seek it; that by next April the Englishmen would arrive with a great armada to lie in wait for, and capture the fleet of New Spain or Nombre de Dios, since perforce it had to pass by here; and that if help did not come, Laudonnière would bring forces and supplies for this, since he had written to France asking for them. The English ships were to come to this coast by April, as has been said; and for this undertaking I found they had in the fort's dockyard, a large galley and seven ships, five of their own and two which they had stolen. They wished to send the four galleons to France to be laden with men and supplies, and they were to join the ships left here by April, together with the Englishmen who would then have arrived also. Jean Ribault, with eight hundred men who were to remain here with him, wanted to go this coming January to Los Mártires, over in front of Havana, about twenty-five leagues from there, and build a fort in that place, for they say they have reconnoitered there a very fine harbor; and from there, when in the summer he should have his whole fleet together, watching for the convoys, he wished to capture Havana. And Your Majesty may be certain that this affair was arranged, concerted, and planned between them; and before Jean Ribault left France, he had orders to fortify himself in Los Martires, over in front of Havana, about twenty-five or thirty leagues distant, so that no ship could pass out of the channel without being seen by him; likewise to keep six galleys there, which is the best sea in the world for them; and thence to capture Havana and give freedom to all those of Hispaniola, Puerto Rico, and all Tierra Firme; for I informed myself of this very sufficiently from the talkative Frenchman whose life I spared. They brought with them six Portuguese as pilots, two of whom were put to the knife, two others were killed by the Indians, and Jean Ribault has the other two with him.

The river by the Fort of San Mateo, which we took from the Frenchmen, goes inland for sixty leagues, and one does not reach the end thereof in the direction of the southwest until it comes out almost at the Bay of Juan Ponce;[8] thence to New Spain and to the port of San Juan de Lua[9] there are not much more than two hundred and fifty leagues. There in that Bay of Juan Ponce they intended to build a fort in the coming year, as it is so near New Spain and Honduras, about one hundred and fifty leagues therefrom, and as many from Yucatan; and whence the six galleys they had could navigate with ease.

On this river there are large settlements of Indians, and they are all great friends of the Frenchmen who went there three times to seek maize; and as they had disembarked here with great lack of supplies, so great that within eight days they had nothing to eat, and there is very little maize along this coast, the French took it by force from the Indians; and as the Indians are more inclined to take than to give, and are a very poor people although very brave, all of them have not such perfect friendship for the French that they cannot have a firmer one with us, for I shall not allow one grain of maize to be taken from them; on the contrary, I shall give them from whatever I have, because it is proper to do so.

Considering these lands to be so extensive, with so good a climate, and the damage and disturbance that the enemies and corsairs can cause in them every day; and that they can take possession of those lands lying north of here where they can easily maintain themselves near Tierra Nova,[10] where they are masters by tyranny--I counsel that the following be carried out by all means. Your Majesty may put aside the thought that it will not be done at the smallest possible cost to Your Majesty; for if any loss occurs, it will be mine. And, therefore, Your Majesty can increase your expenditures as much as you may be pleased, since thus it befits your royal service and the increase of your realms.

This harbor is situated in 29.5 degrees, and that of Fort San Mateo, which we captured, is in 30.25, for the French and their pilots were mistaken, and I have had observations taken by the sun on shore, to verify this. From here to the Cape of Canaveral it is fifty leagues, and three rivers and harbors[11] between, and from there to Havana it is a hundred leagues, more or less, which can be sailed by boats along the islands of Canaveral and Los Mártires, and thence one can cross twenty-five or thirty leagues to Havana and no farther. I have resolved to take two very good pinnaces which I captured from the Frenchmen, with one hundred men, and go along the coast, the boats going by sea, being hauled on shore at night; and inside the Cape of Canaveral, where the sea is like a river, I will search with the boats along the islands of Canaveral and all Los Mártires for the best harbor and fittest place to erect a fort; which will be stronger because of the one at Havana, and the Havana fort will be strengthened by this one. We shall make sure that at no time, within these hundred and fifty leagues that are between here and Havana, will the enemy be able to attack or fortify themselves; or lie in wait for convoys or ships from the Indies; for with the men who are in Havana, those of Santo Domingo, and those of Pedro de las Roelas, I shall have forces enough to do this during March,

when I shall go across in these pinnaces to Havana to seek these people. After I shall have discovered the site for the fort, and Pedro de las Roelas shall have arrived at Havana, he will find his ship there, as I have no intention of taking her from that harbor, and he will find his men; so that he may return to Spain as strong as he was before. I shall place there now one hundred and fifty Spaniards, for they are needed to keep watch over the Indians, who are very warlike, until the Spaniards shall have gained their good will; and at the beginning of April I shall be back in these two forts, as I can return along the seacoast in seven or eight days.

By May it will be necessary for me, after leaving these two forts with the best forces possible, each with three hundred soldiers, to go in boats that draw little water, most of which I shall have ready here--which will be this galley and the French brigantine, and as many of mine as I can take, with five hundred soldiers and one hundred sailors--to settle at Santa Elena,[12] which is fifty leagues from here, and has three harbors and rivers within three leagues; the largest one has six fathoms of water, the other, four; admirable harbors; and the one we call Santa Elena, which is the third, where the Frenchmen were, is very poor. All three can be navigated inland from one to the other, so that whoever is master of one will be master of all

168

three. There, in the best place, I shall build a fort, and leave therein three hundred soldiers who will complete it; and I shall go on thence to the Bay of Santa María,[13] in 37 degrees, one hundred and thirty leagues beyond Santa Elena, which is the land of the Indians of Mexico, and erect another fort and leave therein the other two hundred soldiers.

This must be the key to all the fortifications on these lands, since from there on towards Tierra Nova, there is no place fit for settlement, because to the north of this harbor, eighty leagues within the country, there are mountain ridges, and at the foot of them is an arm of the sea[14] which empties at Tierra Nova, and which can be sailed for six hundred leagues. This arm of the sea enters at Tierra Nova, and ends eighty leagues inland in the territory of the Indians, which is on this Bay of Santa María in 37 degrees; and within a half league there is another arm of salt water going in the direction of west-north-west, which, it is suspected, leads to the South Sea. The Indians slaughter many of the cows[15] of New Spain, which Francisco Vásquez de Coronado found on those plains, and they carry the hides in canoes to Tierra Nova by way of this arm of the sea, and sell them to the Frenchmen in exchange for goods. In the last two years, from these parts, the fishing boats have carried more than six thousand hides to La Rochelle;

and by this arm of the sea the Frenchmen can go with their ships' boats in which they fish, to these lands of the Indians, and they find themselves at the foot of the mountain ridge, four hundred leagues from the mines of San Martín and New Galicia. In order for them to control that land at their pleasure, they had to place their frontiers hither, and gain possession of the Bahama Channel, and then, entering from there, they could make themselves masters of the mines of New Spain. By all and every means it is necessary that Your Majesty should hold and be master of this key and fortress, because then you will be master of Tierra Nova; for if we have galleys in that arm of the sea, no ship will be allowed to fish there unless tribute is paid, and that land is recognized to be Your Majesty's. And all the Indies must be secured; and if the arm of the sea goes to the South Sea, which is held as certain, it is near China, which is an important thing for the enlightenment of those people, and the trade with Molucca. It is for these reasons that it is needful to go this coming May with five hundred soldiers and one hundred sailors to fortify Santa Elena and this Bay of Santa María. I am writing to Pedro del Castillo, who has my power of attorney, to send me at my cost three hundred soldiers, and supplies for them for one year; likewise provisions for another eight hundred persons whom I have here and at

169

Havana, partly soldiers and partly useless people, not counting the three hundred soldiers who are on Your Majesty's account. Your Majesty, at La Mejorada, through your Councils of War and State, provided no cause or reason that they should neglect to pay me. I do not know what Your Majesty may have provided in this matter. I entreat that Your Majesty, if you have not yet commanded that I should be paid, be pleased to have me paid at once, so that I may provide myself with the things requisite and necessary for bringing this enterprise to a successful issue; and that Your Majesty may be pleased to order that these people be provided with the supplies due them on what was allowed them for a year, because we are suffering a great lack of food, and the hardships and dangers we endure are many, for the fort here is being built by working each person, of whatever rank, six hours every day; three hours before noon and three after; and if the people do not stand it well, many will become ill or will die; moreover they will all become discontented, which is a very bad thing. Let Your Majesty order two hundred soldiers besides those Your Majesty has furnished for this enterprise, in such wise that Your Majesty will not pay for more than five hundred altogether, including those who are here and those who are to come, and the one hundred sailors who went to Hispaniola in the galleon, that she might be careened and

remain there in some harbor, ready for active service with all the supplies on board; for if the bread should be landed and exposed to the air, it would all be spoiled; and it would keep in good condition on board, together with the ammunition which we could not land, for fear of the enemy. It was fitting that the hundred sailors and lombarderos[16] on board should be fully prepared to fight, so that if the enemy should go in search of the galleon, they could defend themselves; and therefore I shall send vessels so that during January she can be unloaded. I shall send to pay off the ship and crew from the first of February, so that from the first of February onward Your Majesty can take that amount of tonnage from there, and these hundred sailors and lombarderos, that they may bring the supplies that are to come and the artillery and ammunition, in accordance with the memorandum which goes with this letter; for this is a proper and necessary thing. With these two hundred soldiers who are to come at Your Majesty's expense, and the three hundred who will come at my cost in other ships, I shall carry out my plan for May at Santa Elena and the Bay of Santa Maria, before the French can anticipate me, because it is a thing of the greatest importance; and Your Majesty will certainly find that instead of the five hundred persons I was obliged to place in these parts, I have put one thousand, counting the people I have in Havana, the three hundred that I now ask may be here by April, and two hundred others whom it is fitting should be sent me by the month of October, to settle on the Bay of Juan Ponce; because the river at the Fort of San Mateo, which we took from the enemy, goes inland for sixty leagues from this bay, so that by means of this river one can pass easily from one sea to the other; and the multitude of Indians thereabouts will be thus sooner brought to the knowledge of our holy Catholic faith. On this Bay of Juan Ponce is the province of Apalache whose people are indomitable, and with whom the Spaniards have never been able to do anything; and if that province be a plain, it is probable that it may easily extend as a plain up to New Galicia, a distance of some three hundred leagues, and as many more to Vera Cruz, and as many more to Honduras and Yucatan; and from Yucatan this settlement will be provided with maize, since there is much of it there, in great quantity. And one hundred and fifty leagues inland, towards the north is the Province of Coça, whose people are our friends, in 38 or 39 degrees, at the foot of the mountain ridges which begin near the mines of Zacatecas and San Martín. That province must be about one hundred and fifty leagues away from all our settlements, these forts, the river of Santa Elena, and the land of the Indians; and when, after the year 1565, Coça is settled and a good city built there, there will be nothing more to do but settle in Florida, and it will be easy trading and traveling on the route to New Spain, and we shall benefit greatly from the many silver mines in that country, which are the mines of Zacatecas. Within a few years, even, the silver obtained from those mines and sierras of San Martín will come to these harbors, and to Santa Elena and the Bay of Santa María; because from the mines of Zacatecas and San Martín it is more than two hundred leagues to the harbor of San Juan de Lua, and navigation from that harbor to this is very dangerous and laborious; while the journey to Spain from here, from Santa Elena, and from the Bay of Santa María is easy and short; ordinarily of forty or fifty days. And as for the hundred leagues more of travel on land which there will be from the mines of Zacatecas and San Martín to these harbors, they will prefer to bring the silver here, owing to the short and safe sea voyage, rather than to San Juan de Lua. And from that Bay of Juan Ponce, in the province of Apalache, where we must make a settlement, it is not more than fifty leagues by land to these forts; so that we shall be able to help and communicate with one another very easily from harbor to harbor. As to myself, Your Majesty may be sure that, beyond that for which I am pledged, I shall spend in this undertaking everything I can possibly obtain, earn, and acquire from my kindred and friends, that I may be able to carry it forward and succeed therein; and that the Gospel may be preached to these natives, and they may come to obey Your Majesty. For this I keep watch, and shall watch, by day and by night, with mind and soul, to the best of my ability.

Since these lands are extensive and have many fine rivers and harbors, and the natives of this country are numerous, and so many results cannot be brought about by a few Spaniards, it is not expedient in any way that we should do it gradually, but quickly, and spend in five years what might be spent in ten; for in this manner shall Your Majesty become master of such great provinces, and enlighten the natives thereof, and greatly increase your kingdoms. Because in these lands there will be many very good farms; also much wine, many sugar plantations, a great number of livestock, for there are extensive pastures; much hemp, pitch, tar, and lumber, things which Your Majesty does not have in your kingdoms. Many ships can be built, but as for salt and wheat along these shores, so far as we have seen, there is none; there must be all kinds of fruits, there is very good water, and a very fine climate to the country; there must be much rice, and many pearls in the rivers of Santa Elena, where we have been told they can be found; and entering further into this land, there must be places where much wheat can be obtained and silk produced.

I have need of thirty thousand ducats for the things I am sending to ask for in Spain for these parts--things which are necessary and indispensable, such as supplies and equipment for ships, and clothes and shoes for the people--but I have not one ducat yet. Your Majesty will be pleased to command that the pay for the galleon for all January be paid to me; also that of the hundred men who came in her, together with the supplies due them, for the sailors would not come to these parts for such small pay, so that to bring them I obligated myself to Francisco Duarte; and I made the best bargain I could with them; it is certain that they cost me three thousand ducats over and above what Your Majesty pays them. Your Majesty ordered that I send a ship from Florida with the news of my arrival; since it is my own, I want no freight money. I gave the ship-master, the pilot, and the sailors one thousand ducats for pay and food; Your Majesty will order this paid to me later. As for the rest of the thirty thousand ducats which I need, I am assured by Pedro del Castillo that he will seek them, and will bind himself to provide me with all that I am sending to ask him for; because as he has no children and is a very good Christian, he has taken it upon him as his principal care to aid me with all his means in this enterprise, that I may succeed therein, without his having any further object than to be my friend and to want to help me in a time of such need. I supplicate Your Majesty that for love of Our Lord, you command that what is due me be delivered to me with great promptness, and that those supplies be provided which are for Your Majesty's account; likewise the men's pay, and the pay to be given over there to the two hundred soldiers, so that all may be here during April, and by the beginning of May I may go to Santa Elena and to the Bay of Santa María, which is the outpost and frontier that Your Majesty must hold to be master of these parts; for unless this be done, we shall have done nothing, and if the French set foot there, much money will be spent, and much time must elapse, before they can be driven out from there; and it is not well to treat this matter lightly.

Diego Flores de Valdes, who goes with this dispatch and who will return with the succor asked for, is a gentleman who for fifteen years, in all the fleets under my command, has been serving Your Majesty as a captain of armed ships, and some-times as my lieutenant. He has always served well and with all diligence, and has done the same in this voyage, in which I have made him Admiral of the armada and my lieutenant; and up to this day Your Majesty has never favored him in any way, nor given him any aid toward his expenses, although Ruy Gómez y Eraso offered to do so in Your Majesty's name when I made the voyages to Flanders in the zabras, at which time he was my lieutenant; but nothing was ever paid him. He is in straitened circumstances, and has sold or pledged the greater part of the patrimony he inherited from his ancestors, in the hope, which he always has, that Your Majesty will show him some favor. I have rewarded him but little, because of my own necessities, and I have great need of him to serve Your Majesty in affairs of the sea in these parts, because he knows well how to do it. I beseech Your Majesty to confer on him an order of knighthood, and some aid in defraying his expenses, as it will all be for serving Your Majesty the better; and in order to go with vessels of the armada on the seas along these coasts, it is well to have great authority among enemies and friends, and the knighthood would aid him much. He takes with him two pilots, that they may return with the ships that will bring this succor; one of them is one of the best sailors there is in all these kingdoms, and very prudent; and with him and with those others everything will succeed, well managed and with good report.

As I was writing this, the tenth of this month, news came to me that the fort we had taken from the French had caught fire one night, and all the stores were burned, and everything that had been captured therein. I succored it instantly, dividing with the men who were there the supplies and munitions I had here; and within an hour of my receiving these tidings came another message to me; that Jean Ribault, with two hundred soldiers, was five or six leagues from here, in the place where I worked justice upon the French belonging to the three ships under his charge which had been lost. Fearing that his friends the Indians might join with him, and give me trouble, I went immediately to look for him with one hundred and fifty soldiers, and the next day, at dawn, on the eleventh of this month, I came up with him. As there was a river between us, which could not be crossed except by swimming, both sides made a demonstration of force, each party with two banners displayed, and sounding their fifes and drums. Upon pledge of safety, he sent his sergeant major to speak with me, who brought me a message from Jean Ribault, and all his men, that I should give them safe conduct to their fort. I answered them, as I had the others: that I was their enemy, and was waging a war of fire and blood against them because they were Lutherans, and had come to spread their evil sect in these Your Majesty's dominions, and instruct the Indians therein; and I undeceived him as to his fort, for we had captured it. I said that they might give up their flags and

weapons to me, and put themselves at my mercy, for me to do with their persons as I might wish; and that nothing else could they do or accomplish with me. And the sergeant major having gone with this reply, that same day in the afternoon Jean Ribault came to speak to me, under pledge of entire safety, to treat with me of some conditions more favorable for himself; and as I would not grant any, he said he would return on the morning of the next day with the answer. And so he came back, with almost seventy companions, and many important persons among them; three or four captains and among these, Captain Corceto, who for a long time was captain of arquebusiers in Lombardy; Captain La Grange, who was captain of infantry on land, was already dead. There came also with Jean Ribault, among these people, four Germans, relatives of the Prince of Orange, great Lutherans. I wished to ascertain if there were any Catholic among them, but not one was found. I spared the lives of two young gentlemen of about eighteen years, and of three others, who were a fifer, a drummer, and a trumpeter. I had Jean Ribault, with all the rest, put to the knife, understanding this to be expedient for the services of God Our Lord and of Your Majesty; and I hold it very great good fortune that he should be dead; for the King of France could do more with him with fifty thousand ducats, than with others with five hundred thou-

174

sand; and he could do more in one year than another in ten, for he was the most experienced seaman and corsair known, and very skillful in this navigation of the Indies and the coast of Florida. He was so friendly with England, and had such a reputation in that kingdom, that he was named Captain-General of the whole English armada against the Catholics of France during these past years, when there was war between England and France. The other people whom Jean Ribault had with him, who might have been about seventy or eighty persons, fled to the woods, for they would not surrender unless I granted them their lives. These, with twenty others who escaped from the fort, and fifty others the Indians captured from the wrecked ships, in all one hundred and fifty persons, rather less than more, are all the Frenchmen alive today in Florida, separated from one another and fleeing in the woods, and others captives of the Indians. And because they are Lutherans, and in order that such an evil sect may not survive in these parts, I shall so strive for my part, and induce the Indians my friends to do so on theirs, that within five or six months very few, if any, will remain alive; and of the thousand French who had landed when I arrived in these provinces, with their fleet of twelve sails, two ships only have escaped, badly damaged, with forty or fifty people on board. As they are ill-provided and equipped,

they may not reach France; and if these should arrive, they would not bring news of the death of Jean Ribault and the destruction of his armada; the later they come to know of this in France, the better it will be, because their minds are at rest, thinking they have strong forces here. And now it is more necessary than ever that everything I ask for be provided with great diligence and secrecy, so that it may be here during April, and the coming summer I can gain control of this coast of Florida, and thus Your Majesty will soon be master thereof, without opposition or anxiety; and being master of Florida, you will secure the Indies and the navigation thereto. And I assure Your Majesty that henceforth you can sustain Florida at very little cost, and it will yield Your Majesty much money, and will be worth more to Spain than New Spain, or even Peru. It can be said that this land is a suburb of Spain; for in truth, it took me no more than forty days of sailing to come to it, and ordinarily as many more are necessary to return to those kingdoms. Owing to the burning of the fort, we endure very great hunger, as the flour was burned, and the biscuit that I brought here is becoming stale and giving out. If we are not succored soon, we shall suffer, and many will pass away from this world from starvation; but trusting that Your Majesty is sure that I am serving you with fidelity and love, and that in everything

I am dealing truthfully and shall continue to do so, I say no more, except that I shall advise Your Majesty, in every way I can, of all that may occur. May Our Lord keep and cause to prosper the royal Catholic person of Your Majesty, with the extension of greater kingdoms and dominions, as Christianity has need thereof, and we, Your Majesty's servants, desire. From these provinces of Florida, on the beach of San Pelayo and Fort of St. Augustine, on the fifteenth of October in the year 1565.

Your Majesty's humble servant, who kisses your royal hands.

P. Menéndez

NOTES

1. Archivo General de Indias, Seville. This letter was translated from a copy (Connor Papers, Library of Congress) of the original at Seville. Other copies are in the Colección Navarrete, Depósito Hidrográfico, Madrid; Woodbury Lowery Collection, Library of Congress; and the Buckingham Smith Collection, New York Historical Society. The letter is published in Ruidíaz, *La Florida*, II, 84-105; a translation is in the *Proceedings of the Massachusetts Historical Society*, 2d Series, VIII, 425-39.

In the letter of Menéndez to King Philip II, dated from the beach of San Pelayo, Fort of St. Augustine, October 15, 1565, he relates his capture of the Fort of San Mateo (Fort Caroline) with everything in it; he gives advice as to the measures to be taken to become master and owner of that region, describes the region, and tells of the wealth to be found in it; he begs for soldiers and money; he receives word that the fort taken from the Frenchmen has burned to the ground, and sets out to help it; he writes of the capture and death of Jean Ribault and 200 Frenchmen.

2. " . . . su borracha de açumbre y medio y de dos." An *azumbre* was a half-gallon measure.

3. First Menéndez speaks of three ships up the river near the fort, then of two. Solís de Merás speaks of three; Le Moyne says that the *Pearl* of Jacques Ribault was the only vessel taken up as far as the fort. The letter of Menéndez and Mendoza's "Memoir" confirm this latter statement to the extent of saying that two of the seven ships from France were a league farther down the river at the time Fort Caroline was captured.

4. "Pidiome que el yria con esta enbaxada y de noche se bolveria a nado, que le otorgase a el la vida: yo lo hize por ver que tratava verdad y me podia alunbrar de muchas cosas: y luego que fue buelto a sus compañeros, vino un gentilonbre Lugarteniente del musiur ludunier, muy ladino en estas partes, para tentarme: y abiendo dado y tomado conmigo, ofreciome que me entregarian las armas y se darian, con que les otorgase la vida: respondile que las armas me podia rendir, y ponerse debaxo de mi gracia, para que yo hiziese dellos aquello que nuestro señor me ordenase, y de aqui no me saco ni sacara si dios nuestro señor no espirara en mi otra cosa: y ansi se fue con esta rrespuesta, y se vinieron y me entregaron las armas, y hizeles amarrar las manos atras y pasarlos a cuchillo." Ruidíaz, II, 85.

5. Chaplain Mendoza speaks of 10 or 12 Frenchmen as being saved, then on the same page he says 14 or 15. Solís de Merás says that only 8 were spared. Solís and Barrientos agree that 208 Frenchmen had their hands tied behind their backs.

This entire page of the letter, to Note 6, is missing in Ruidíaz.

6. Here ends the passage in the original letter which is missing in Ruidíaz.

7. In Mexico, then called New Spain.

8. Menéndez had got an idea from the Indians that by means of the St. Johns River he could travel nearly to the west coast of the Florida peninsula. The Bay of Juan Ponce, also called the Bay of Carlos, is now Charlotte Harbor.

9. San Juan de Ulloa, off Veracruz.

10. Newfoundland.

11. By "harbors" he here means Matanzas Inlet; a smaller inlet, near it, which has been closed up for the past hundred years, and was called, after Ribault, the Barreta de Ribao and also the Barreta del Peñon; and finally Mosquito Inlet.

12. Near Port Royal, South Carolina.

13. Chesapeake Bay.

14. Lake Erie, Lake Ontario, and the St. Lawrence River.

15. Probably buffaloes.

16. The gunners who worked an early piece of ordnance called a *lombarda*.

CATHERINE DE MEDICI, mother of young King Charles IX of France and Regent of the Kingdom, wrote from the royal estates at Moulins, France, to the French Ambassador to Spain, Raymond Fourquevaux. The letter was published in *Lettres de Cathérine de Médicis* (Paris, 1880), vol. II, and the translation was made by the late Jeannette Thurber Connor. The letter is in the Connor Papers at the Library of Congress and is published with the Library's permission.

Letter from Catherine de Medici

efore the Ambassador of Spain had sent his courier your first packet arrived, of which your other dispatch makes mention, whereby I was very particularly informed how that unfortunate massacre perpetrated in Florida took place and what were the remarks concerning it made to you by the Duke of Alba, with the good and pertinent reply you made thereto, and such as a case so cruel and inhuman required. I did not wish to noise it about, nor let it be known that I knew anything until yesterday, when the said Ambassador, having asked for an audience with the King, Monsieur my son, and with me, came to see us, and after many other subjects he brought up, he told us he was charged by his master, Monsieur my son-in-law, to advise us that there had arrived in Spain a captain bringing tidings that Pierre Melendez-having found in the land of Florida a few Frenchmen avowed by and bearing letters from Monsieur the Admiral, who had in their company a few ministers who were implanting the new religion there--had chastised them, as he

said he had orders to that effect from the King his master. He did confess that it had been accomplished a little more roughly and cruelly than his said master would have desired, but that he could do no less than to fall upon them as pirates and people who were there to attempt to seize that which belonged to him. (The Ambassador) said that notwithstanding, the King his master demanded justice on the said Admiral. The King, my son, who was still in bed, rather weak from the illness he had had--from which he has recovered, thanks to God--wished that I should give him a reply. It was this: That I had already been fully apprised of the facts by a man who had returned to us from there, and as the common mother,* I could only feel at heart an unspeakable sorrow on hearing that although these princes are such friends, allied and related, as these two kings are, with such peace between them, and at a time when we shall observe towards (the Spaniards) so many and such great offices of friendship, such a horrible carnage should have been committed on the subjects of the King my said son, to whom, up to then, I had not wished to speak thereof, on account of his illness. That I was as if beside myself when I thought thereon, and could not persuade myself that the King his master would not give us reparation and justice. For there is no ground to fasten this on the said Admiral, as it is surely credible that he did not let so many people go out of this kingdom without the sanction of the King my son, who considers that commerce and navigation are everywhere free to his subjects. And that land where the deed was committed is not (Philip's), but was discovered by our subjects so long since, that it still bears the name (of the Terre des Bretons), as his ministers likewise have already been notified by you. And even though they had gone into the very countries of the King his master, acting otherwise than they should between friends, Spaniards should have contented themselves with taking them prisoners and returning them to the King my son, to have them punished if they had done wrong, instead of using them thus; (wherefore) I could not believe that he would not give us satisfaction. That it seemed as if they wanted to curb the King my son, shut him up in this kingdom and clip his wings, a thing which he could not suffer, and would not be advised so to do; giving him thereby a reason for thinking and providing otherwise in his affairs: as he will know well how to do, if God please, and the means do not fail him; in such wise that I hoped

he would have no consideration for his neighbors, and would no more respect them than they do him. That his kingdom, thank God, was at peace, and he better obeyed than he ever was; wherefore it could be readily believed that it will not be difficult for him to make those who would do him a wrong feel and know that he has no less means to protect himself against it than had the Kings his predecessors. The said Ambassador continued to try to charge the act upon the Admiral, and (said) that there were ministers of the religion there, which was a thing most displeasing to his master; but I said to him that we did not inquire what people were going on the said voyage, and that if wishes were realized, I should want all the Huguenots to be in that country, where he cannot justly say that he has any interest, since the land is ours, as we lay claim thereto; (he is) making us see that they care little for the peace of this kingdom, since they thus want to take from us the means of establishing it here;* but however that may be, it is not for them to punish our subjects, and we do not dispute as to whether they were of the religion or not, but as to the murder (the Spaniards) committed on them, of which it is very reasonable that his master should order the justice we ask of him given to us. To which it seemed to me the Ambassador was much at a loss what to answer, and to strengthen his complaints he spoke to us of Corsica likewise whither he says that many boats ordinarily go from Provence laden with supplies, munitions and people, whereof the Genoese complained; as to which I satisfied him very well, and said that these are the usual impostures. He likewise spoke to me of a few galleys which he says are being armed in Marseilles, which I admitted, for they protect our coasts, infested, as they are, by an infinite number of corsairs whom his (the Catholic King's) very quarrel brings us there; amd whom we have been mildly enduring out of consideration for him. When all is said, he had amassed a world of complaints to give color to that of Florida, to which there is as little foundation; but what he took away with him is that he realized well that we have taken this in very ill part, and he does not think we will forget it. This I have been willing to write to you at length, for the King my son: praying and ordering what you may make it well understood to the Catholic King, praying him very affectionately that for the sake of duty and reason, he render the justice and reparation which such an enormous wrong deserves, by some demonstration worthy of the friendship and peace which exists between us; and that he should consider the injury he would be doing it if he should not give us the satisfaction which the King my son expects, and which I desire on my part, for I shall never be well content nor at my ease, until

I believe it to be in conformity with the sincerity of our affection for, and our actions towards him, whereof it would grieve me too much that advantage should be taken; and I should have the deepest regret at having wasted so much pain and care, and sought every means to nurture these two princes and their crowns in perpetual amity (if I were to find), that instead of the good I hoped to see resulting therefrom, the King, my son, should reproach me some day, saying that while he had rested his affairs on me, I had allowed such a stain to be made on his reputation: whereon I pray you that by your first dispatch I may be enlightened, feeling assured that the said Ambassador will forget to make known nothing of what I have said to him in the matter, and of the wrong (the Catholic King) is doing to the well-being I seek for this kingdom; for to speak to you frankly, I believe that the Huguenots who are within it could not have asked for better news, knowing thereby that the friendship we look for from that side (the Catholic King) is very ill assured, since our subjects are thus treated; which I hope that God will not leave unpunished, as I wish you to make the Queen my daughter understand very well, besides what I am writing to her thereon, and to show her this letter, if she wishes to see it. I have seen, moreover, what you write to me on the subject of the marriages, whereof I am no longer thinking. The King my son is young enough to wait for something better, and such a great prince that it cannot be but that he will always be able to choose throughout all Christendom, whatever hindrance thereto one may think of using, as I know and realize that one is doing this.* I pray God, Monsieur de Forquevaux, that He may have you in His holy keeping.

Written at Moulins the XVII day of March, 1566.

Caterine

I cannot refrain from telling you that although a number of other matches offer themselves for the King my son, and among these the greatest in Christendom, the very greatest regret I have is that it may be necessary in the end, because of the wrong being done him, that he choose some one who will not be of our religion; which we shall only do if we are pushed to extremity.

The Revenge of Captain Gourgues

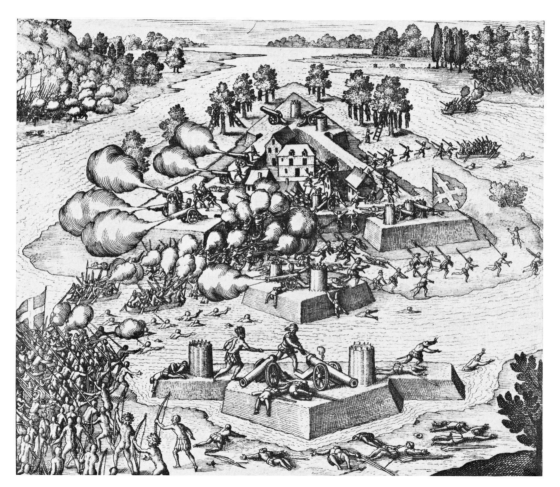

Gourgues captures San Mateo, 1568

THE PRINCIPAL DOCUMENT of the French experience in Florida that has never been published in a complete English translation is an account of the revenge inflicted in 1568 on the Spaniards in Florida by Captain Dominique de Gourgues. An abridged version of "La Reprinse de la Floride par le capitaine Gourgues" was published in M. M. Basanier, *L'Histoire notable de la Floride* (Paris, 1586). This version was translated and published in Richard Hakluyt, *A Notable Historie Containing Foure Voyages Made by Certaine French Captaynes into Florida* (London, 1587). Complete French versions appeared in Henri Ternaux-Compans, *Recueil de pièces sur la Floride* (Paris, 1841), Tamizey de Larroque, *La Reprinse de la Floride* (Paris, 1867), Paul Gaffarel, *Histoire de la Floride française* (Paris, 1875), and Charles de La Roncière, *La Floride française* (Paris, 1928).

The present English version was translated in the 1920's by Mrs. Jeannette Thurber Connor. She introduced it by the only existing biography of Gourgues. In her plan it was to be the final item in two volumes of reproductions of French documents; of these only Jean Ribault, *The Whole and True Discouerye of Terra Florida,* was published during her lifetime. It is now available in the Floridiana Facsimile and Reprint Series (University of Florida Press, Gainesville, 1964).

Five variant manuscripts of the "Reprinse de la Floride" exist in the Bibliothèque Nationale at Paris (Fonds Français 20794, 2145, 3884, 19899, and 20994). Copies of these were furnished Mrs. Connor by Charles Samaran, the distinguished French scholar, and with his aid she based her translation on Fr 20794, but carefully collated it with the others.

The original of the biography and translation are in the Connor Papers at the Library of Congress. They are published with the permission of the Library of Congress.

The Connor Biography

WHEN FLORIDA seemed hopelessly lost to France, when after the Floridian massacres the French Court turned the deafest of ears to the indignation of the French nation, a man appeared on the scene who was destined to be regarded as one of the world's heroes. Laudonnière was a good seaman and a charming writer; Ribault was a great seaman; Menéndez was a great man; but Dominique de Gourgues was essentially a hero.

Born about 1530 in Mont-de-Marsan, Gascony, he was "the Catholic gentleman who took upon himself, at his own expense, risk, and peril, to avenge the death of the Huguenots in Florida." In his early youth there was general fighting going on in most European countries, and Dominique de Gourgues fought the Spaniards in Italy, where among other feats he, with twenty men, sustained a siege against a whole Spanish company. They were captured after a magnificent resistance, the garrison was butchered, and Gourgues was chained to the bench of a Spanish galley. It was there that first grew up within him his deep-seated, never-ending hatred of the Spaniard. The vessel on which he was a prisoner was afterward captured by the Turks, but Gourgues continued to be a galley slave. The ship was later taken by Mathurin de Lescout, the Sieur de Romégas, Commander of the Knights of Malta, and Gourgues, free at last, returned to France. Travels and adventures followed for him, on the coast of Africa, in Brazil, in the seas of the Indies; then he served in France in the cause of the Guises. This last fact alone should refute the contention of Spanish historians, and some French ones, that Gourgues was a Huguenot. He was in reality a good Roman Catholic but a still more fervent patriot, the crowning achievement of whose life was to avenge the Spanish outrage on French Protestants in Florida. The researches, over sixty years ago, of the Viscount Alexis de Gourgues,[1] although not proof positive, went far towards showing that his ancestor was a member of the Church of Rome. More recently the works of Maurice Delpeuch[2] and Charles de La Roncière[3] have added much to the knowledge of Gourgues' life and deeds, but in 1911 an article was published in Paris which definitely established that Dominique de Gourgues was a Roman Catholic.[4] This was done by the study of his will.

It was in 1567-68 that Dominique de Gourgues, one man in a great nation, raised the little expedition that effaced the blot on the honor of France.

In Spain in the year 1567 the Adelantado Pedro Menéndez was giving an account of his voyages to Florida, and writing a report for the Council of the Indies in which he petitioned for a grant of appropriations to pay his debts in order that all he had spent in the service of Philip II might be reimbursed him. His return to America was so delayed that the time was auspicious for French reprisals, if there could be any in spite of the government's fear of Spain. Barcia's way of describing the situation is that the Huguenots, "with a thousand lies and inventions, each person relating a rare and odious case" of the Spaniards' cruelties to the poor Frenchmen in Florida, "finally persuaded and secretly helped Dominique de Gourgues of Mont-de-Marsan (a terrible heretic) to sail over to avenge the injury done to his accursed sect in the justice worked on Ribault and his companions."[5]

The truth was that no one had been influencing Gourgues. He needed no urging and had no assistance but his brother's. He borrowed on his property to carry out his project (some authors say he sold it), and was generously helped by his brother, who was Ogier de Gourgues, President of the Treasurers of France in the Generality of Guyenne. On Dominique's return from America, he was received with enthusiasm in La Rochelle and Bordeaux. The Seigneur Montluc, in Bordeaux, bought of him for the town fortifications his captured artillery pieces from Florida. The bill of sale is still in existence. Gourgues, however, did not have time to receive the amount paid for them, for King Philip of Spain had set a price upon his head. He owed certain obligations for the supplies and equipment of his ships, and his troubles began. At this point his brother again came to his assistance.[6]

But the bitterest of disappointments was in store for him. If ever a man had deserved the gratitude of his King and his country, it was Dominique de Gourgues—and he was notified not to appear at court. Spanish influence was preponderant there, and Catherine de Medici and Charles IX (although they were pleased at the Florida events; Alava wrote to Philip that Catherine's manner "showed her great joy") gave no mark of their appreciation to Gourgues himself. He had placed them in an embarrassing position with Philip of Spain.

Here, fortunately, Admiral de Coligny's great voice was heard in indignant protest. Philip wanted Gourgues punished; the Cardinal de Lorraine in open council was laying stress on King Philip's side of the case, endeavoring to make the attack on Florida appear as a declaration of war on Spain, and most of the members of the Council were on the point "of declaring themselves," says Paul Gaffarel, "against the avenger of their outraged native land."[7] They would have done so "had not monsieur de Chastillon [Coligny], with his severe manner, full of gravity, pointed out that if Gourgues had had so much courage that he had undertaken, he alone, that which all France should have done, he deserved a great reward and not a punishment; and that those who condemned him for such a generous deed seemed already to want to reduce us to shameful vassalage to our capital enemy; so that even King Charles IX, who was courageous, was moved in his youthfulness; and you could not believe how much honor and glory the decree which followed brought to the Admiral, even in the mouths of the foreign ambassadors who were at court."[8] Dupleix says: "Gourgues was so well defended by the principal personages at court, and particularly by the Admiral, that his Majesty and his Council decided that in avenging his own wrongs, he had also avenged those of France."[9]

In spite of Coligny's warm championship of Gourgues, and of the praise given his conduct by the contemporary historians d'Aubigné and de Thou, there was no public recognition of the entire country's obligation to him. Indeed, during the year 1570 he lived in hiding, with the assistance of two friends, but he was too good a Frenchman to complain. According to a manuscript in the Bibliothèque Nationale, Paris,[10] the King of Spain set a price on Gourgues' head and begged Charles IX to make short work of him.

Whether Gourgues kept in seclusion for a year is doubtful, for two months after his return from Florida he was given the command of a royal galley. And on January 6, 1569, he gave power of attorney to his brother Ogier, "to receive from messieurs the mayors and jurats [of Bordeaux] the sum of 7,500 livres tournois which the said Sieurs owe him, it is said, for the sale made to them of nine pieces of artillery." Yet it is a fact that Gourgues did remain hidden for a while to avoid the assassins in the pay of the Spanish ambassador. Delpeuch suggests that it might have been the skillful Catherine herself who arranged that he should keep in hiding, so as to protect him from King Philip, her son-in-law.[11]

After the Peace of Saint-Germain, in 1570, which put an end to the third War of Religion, Charles IX went over body and soul to the Protestant party. "The amazed courtiers vowed the King would become a Huguenot."[12] The Guises retired from court. Admiral de Coligny was once more master of the situation, and the king called him his father.

Gourgues concealed himself in Paris during a part of 1570, "in a house called la Cour de Rouen," says the manuscript, "situated near the gate of Saint Germain des Près, assisted by the favor of President Marigny, and all his needs being succored by Receiver de Vaquieux on behalf of a relative of the said Gourgues who never forsook him or denied him help from his means." He found himself obliged to accept the aid of President Marigny, "in whose house he remained several days." Charles Samaran's careful perusal of the manuscript enabled him to call attention to a mistake made by La Popelinière in his *Trois Mondes,* and Basanier in his short version of Gourgues' voyage to Florida, a mistake copied by a long line of historians who

189

followed them, including the modern Gaffarel. They all thought that the unfortunate Gourgues had taken refuge in Rouen, with President Marigny, or somewhere else in Normandy; whereas it will not be difficult for those who truly know and love Paris to remember "a very picturesque little passage, composed of a triple court which connects the Rue du Jardinet with the Cour du Commerce. It owes its name to the *hôtel* of the Archbishop of Rouen that stood there in bygone days, and it deserves a visit still, for one sees there the base of a turret which formed a part of the wall of Philip Augustus. Between the much frequented Rue Saint-André-des-Arts and the noisy Boulevard Saint Germain, this is a corner of old Paris forgotten, as it were, and nearly deserted at all hours of the day. Today, like three and a half centuries ago, one might go there for a retreat of calm and silence."[13]

In 1571 one of Gourgues' friends, François de Noailles, Bishop of Acqs, advocated the conquest of Ireland in a Memoir presented to the King's brother, the Duke of Anjou, afterwards Henri III, and proposed that Philippe Strozzi, a very able soldier who was Queen Catherine's cousin, and Dominique de Gourgues should head the army. The Bishop's ambition was to extend in that way France's colonial possessions. "Behind England lies another Peru," wrote he from Lyons on August 16, " . . . that is the kingdom of Ireland . . . one of the best countries in the world, and the most Catholic; the climate is always very temperate, the country is full of mines and metals, and the Queen of England does not hold the fourteenth part thereof: all the rest is held by an infinite number of savage kings that the English have never known how to subdue . . . and if it should not have the aid of ships and men from England, I am willing to lose my noble rank and the dignity I hold in God's church, if the Sieur de Strossy and Captain Gourgues, with seven or eight thousand French arquebusiers, eight hundred or one thousand horses, and six pieces of artillery, do not in less than a year make the whole conquest of that kingdom: which, well regulated and organized, will in less than twenty years after its subjection, yield a greater revenue than that of England."[14]

Nothing came of this unique project which at least showed how high was the opinion of Gourgues' ability, since as a commander he was ranked with Strozzi; that is, as one of the two men in France capable of succeeding in the enterprise.

As time went on, Gourgues continued to be in the royal favor, for a legal paper of March 14, 1572, concerning a large sale of biscuit supplies made to him, speaks of him as being then a gentlemen of the King's Bedchamber.[15] A month afterward, on April 13, Charles IX, at the request of Henri, King of Navarre (who was to become the great and good Henri IV of France), granted Gourgues by letters patent a company of one hundred foot soldiers, in recognition of "the reputation, trustworthiness, ability, valor, experience, capacity, good conduct, and diligence of Captain Gourgues."[16] On May 11 King Henri of Navarre wrote as follows to Dominique: "Captain Gourgues, I have had sent to you the *lettres d'attache*[17] for which you asked me in order to raise your company. I have assigned you the post of Sainte Marie and Marmande wherein to assemble the said company. You shall have a care as long as it is there, that it conduct itself as peaceably as shall be possible, to the great relief of the people; which I feel certain that you will do. I should have been very glad to see you had your health permitted it, assuring you that you would have been welcome, as you always will be when you shall come to see me; and whenever I have the opportunity I shall let you see the good will I feel toward you so whole-heartedly by that I pray God to have you in His holy and worthy keeping. Signed: Your good friend Henri." Comments Delpeuch on this letter, "And one can understand how the Huguenot Henri of Navarre, who knew men, must have held in singular esteem that Catholic who had risked his life and his fortune to avenge the murder of a few of his [Henri's] co-religionists."[18]

Since the year 1568 Charles IX had been assembling a large and mysterious fleet, the destination of which was, and is, unknown. Its departure was deferred time and again, and it was a source of anxiety to Philip of Spain and the other neighbors of Charles, and to the Huguenot city of La Rochelle which thought that these preparations were marks of hostility toward it. Gourgues was to command a large vessel in this fleet and his order for biscuit supplies in March, 1572, is thereby explained. That ship was none other than the *Charles,* about four to five hundred tons, the finest ship in the Royal French Navy. He was to command it for many years. On September 14, 1572, three weeks after the Massacre of St. Bartholomew's Day, Charles IX wrote: "Captain Gourgues, Because of what I have written to my cousin, the Sieur de Strozzi, that I was pleased that he was permitting you to sail by common consent of the whole company, in order to go on a voyage of discovery: I consider that this letter will find you ready to set sail. On your departure, I pray you to be warned not to put in at any place belonging to the King my brother-in-law, or to any princes who are my friends and with whom I am at peace. If you wish me to be satisfied, you shall, above all, fear to disobey me, as I have greater need than I ever had to keep the friendship of my neighbors: govern yourself therefore wisely, and according to my intention, and I will reward the service you shall render me. Praying God, Captain, to have you in His keeping."

Charles had vividly in mind Dominique de Gourgues' attack four years earlier on the Spaniards in Florida, and so admonished him to keep within bounds. The tone of his letter, written as it was just after the massacre, gives ample evidence, says Viscount Alexis de Gourgues, that the King's purpose was no longer to disturb the Protestants in La Rochelle, and La Roncière writes that the choice of Gourgues as the scout of the squadron certainly pointed to some important operation beyond the seas. The latter goes into many details about that elaborate naval expedition which never started. One plan was that a kingdom might be found in Florida for the King's brother, the Duke of Anjou, "the eternal pretender" and seeker after kingdoms. Different cities and individuals were to furnish the ships to the number of one hundred, with six or seven thousand arquebusiers, seventy-two artillery pieces, and agricultural implements of all kinds. Strozzi, Lur-Saluces, and Gourgues on the Charles ran into debt to equip their vessels and secure enthusiastic followers, numbers of them being Huguenots. La Roncière mentions, apparently in connection with this adventure, René de Laudonnière, who was about to start on his second voyage on the *Comtesse Testu*, in partnership with a company of merchants; but it is not made plain that he and his associates had anything to do directly with the project of the great fleet.[19] Its date of clearance was finally set for August 29, 1572. On August 24, the massacre took place. France lost Coligny by his brutal murder that day, and Philip of Spain rejoiced. Had he not written "This Admiral is the poison of the realm and the inventor and promoter of everything evil in it"?[20] In spite of King Charles' letter to Gourgues on September 14, which was subsequent to the St. Bartholomew massacre and alluded to an immediate sailing, Dominique did not sail but was obliged to give up his dreams of colonization with the hope that the Duke of Anjou might take them up at a more auspicious time.[21]

The Calvinists who escaped from the massacre took refuge in their strongholds, especially in La Rochelle, where Captain François de la Noue commanded. The outstanding event of the fourth War of Religion the following winter, spring, and early summer was the siege of La Rochelle, in which Gourgues on board the *Charles* took a prominent, though reluctant, part. At about that period he had also fought with his cousin Anthoine, at the recapture of Blaye, where Anthoine was killed.[22]

By December 4, the city of La Rochelle was besieged on land by Strozzi and Baron de Biron with eight thousand men, while Dominique de Gourgues was to invest it by sea. The Baron de La Garde wrote to him to sail to another point and give up his post, because of the expected arrival of a number of English ships to the assistance of La Rochelle, and Gourgues' reply on February 1, 1573, is exceptionally fine:

"M. de La Garde has now sent to tell me that seventeen warships will arrive from England at night to enter the harbor of La Rochelle; and has ordered me, as soon as I shall sight them, to set sail and go to Brouaige which I do not wish to do. Honor commands us not to desert the road so timorously, and if you will please order the two other ships (the *Anjou* and the *Henry*) to remain near me and give them soldiers, we shall fight them and prevent their entering if the galleys will do their duty."[23]

Gourgues had very little artillery, and the galleys, instead of supporting him, were careful to keep to the south. His letter created a sensation at court; six vessels from Normandy were to be sent to his rescue, but it was discovered when they were about to be dispatched that even in the arsenal at Paris there was no artillery to arm them. Strozzi, meantime, came forward to fight by the side of Gourgues, and Lur-Saluces, the Viscount d'Uza, was sent for in haste from Bordeaux, with his single ship if need be, if the five others of the squadron were not ready. The Baron de La Garde, angry at the turn of affairs and at the position in which he was placed by Gourgues' letter, vowed on his head that nothing should get into La Rochelle.

They did reach it, however, by means of four Protestant ships from Poitou which ran the blockade, led by one fisherman from La Rochelle, called Mirault. At this time the new Lieutenant-General,

Henri, Duke of Anjou, was put in command of the Catholic forces. The English allies of the Huguenots were not ready to appear until the middle of April. The Calvinists had armed all the vessels they had been able to secure on the French coast, and had sent them to Falmouth to join the English fleet; but a little Catholic patache had managed to slip in among them, and as soon as her captain could find out the enemy's date of sailing, he hastened to La Rochelle to warn the Catholic besiegers, who therefore had plenty of time to strengthen the blockade. All along the coast of Brittany, Poitou, and Saintonge burned the beacons, the Catholic signals, to which watchers set fire one after another as the British squadron hove in sight.

On April 19, fifteen large English ships advanced single file toward the harbor of La Rochelle, headed by the *Primrose* and commanded by the Vice-Admiral of Cornwall, Lord Henry Champernon and his father-in-law, Count de Montgomery. The battery at Chef de Baye opened fire: the *Primrose* at the outset was penetrated from side to side by one shot. The French squadron of eighteen vessels and four galleys was under the orders of Vice-Admiral de Lur-Saluces, Viscount d'Uza, on his ship, the *Grand Biscaïen;* it was spread out in order of battle with a buoy in front of each vessel to keep them all on a straight line. Three French ships, under Dominique de Gourgues, remained on guard in the narrow channel at the entrance, and d'Uza signaled him to join the rest of the fleet. Here Gourgues committed "a grave error," writes Delpeuch, "which in our time would be rightfully judged with the upmost severity. But one must also admit that in all countries, this kind of error has always aroused popular enthusiasm. He absolutely refused to obey the orders of his chief and to fall back before the English squadron. And during many hours, seconded only by the batteries of the island of Ré, Gourgues with his three ships withstood the fire of the whole English fleet, and although the cross, the banner of England, still kept advancing the more to surprise the French, as near as within cannon range of the royal squadron, the imperturbable Gourgues continued to fire from all his guns until the receding tide compelled the English fleet to go out to sea and anchor near its coast."

This delay, caused by the tide, the heroism of Gourgues and others, the firm stand of the whole French squadron, and the indecision of Montgomery and Champernon, gave the French an advantage which was strengthened during the night by their receiving substantial reinforcements. Next day the English council of war decided on a temporary retirement, and during the night of April 21 the English fleet sailed away and did not return.

The situation at the siege of La Rochelle between the French Calvinists and the English on the one side, and the French Catholics on the other, had by the month of June, 1573, become a desperate tangle. The city had reached the end of its endurance when five ships of light draft and one bark were able to get through the blockade with supplies and munitions. The Catholic Vice-Admiral, Lur-Saluces, Viscount d'Uza, was made ill by this shock and he did not survive it. More than twenty thousand men of the Catholic army had already died from illness, fatigue, exposure. There were dissensions among the chiefs, and the Duke of Anjou was weary of the struggle. His election to the throne of Poland came as a welcomed means of saving appearances, and being in a happy frame of mind—he had found a kingdom at last!—he raised the siege.

In order to go to Poland, the Duke needed ships and soldiers; "forty vessels, two thousand, one hundred sailors, and four thousand soldiers would take him to Danzig in three weeks' navigation," he wrote to his mother, Queen Catherine.[24] On July 2, King Charles, from Gaillon, sent the following letter to Dominique de Gourgues: "Captain Gourgues, As I have decided to use for the embarkation of 4,000 soldiers, who are to pass over to Poland, some of the largest and best ships of my sea army before the city of La Rochelle, among which is the *Charles* which pertains to you, I have bethought myself to send you these presents at once so that you may be apprised of my intention, requesting you above all that as much as you care for the good of my service, you will see that as soon as possible your vessel is put in readiness so that she can make the aforesaid voyage; having her taken and conducted to Havre de Grâce where she must arrive on the twelfth or thirteenth of the coming month of August; and because it is expedient that she shall be able to come there with the more safety, I beg you to have your ship join those which are likewise ordered to make the said voyage, that she may go in company to the said Havre; all of them together on this occasion going to Bordeaux where the Sieur de Berre is to embark twelve cannon and the other arms which are also to be taken to the said Havre, with all diligence, acting in such wise that they may receive in this matter the service I hope for from you. Praying God that He may have you in His holy keeping."

Here comes one of the gaps in Gourgues' career, for nothing is known of his journey to Poland, if indeed he went there. In the archives of the Department of the Gironde there is a paper dated six months later, January 4, 1574, according to which a sailor by the name of Jehan Roubin promised Dominique de Gourgues, gentlemen in ordinary of the King's Bedchamber, "to keep faithfully well, during the space of three months, for the sum of _____, the king's vessel called the *Charles* . . . during which time the said Sieur Roubin shall be required to take care of the said ship and likewise to see that no cable be stolen, and that the anchors be raised every month. . . ."

Charles IX died on May 30, 1574, devoured with remorse for the Massacre of St. Bartholomew's Day, and the Duke of Anjou left his experiment as King of Poland to become Henri III of France.

A paper preserved in the archives of the Gourgues family, dated the last day of April, 1579, concerns a payment of 7,000 crowns ordered to be made to Dominique de Gourgues by letters patent of Henri III, August 10, 1578, "because of the service rendered by him to the King, at the siege of La Rochelle as well as with his ships and pataches called the *Charles* and the *Desperada*. . . ."

Several years after, he was to command an expedition against Philip II, who had just conquered Portugal, and was to try to restore that kingdom to its rightful owner, Antônio de Crato. According to an interesting anonymous statement quoted by a contemporary French writer, La Popelinière, "he was sought after for his virtues by the Queen of England, and finally chosen by the King our sovereign Lord, and by the King of Portugal, as a man worthy and capable of exercising the charge of admiral in the sea army newly organized by their majesties. He accepted it at the age of sixty years, and departed for Paris. Continuing his voyage to decide some business in Tours with certain lords from Portugal, he was stricken in the said place with an illness, whereof he died. His reputation is such that at present, in this whole kingdom, there is not his equal."

It was evidently a short time before the launching of the undertaking that Gourgues decided to make his will, for he did so on December 5, 1581. Possibly he had a premonition of his approaching end; the year of his death has been proved by Samaran to be 1582. The will was made in Paris, at the house of his friend, Pierre de Vaquieux, in the Rue des Prouxaires.[25] Gourgues was then living in the Rue des Petits-Champs, in a house which had a deer's antlers for a sign. "Considering wisely in himself," says the old document, "that nothing is more certain than death or more uncertain than the day and hour thereof . . . he made his will and disposed of his said worldly goods, in the name of the Father, and of the Son, and of the blessed Holy Ghost, in the manner which followeth:

"And, firstly, as a Christian and Catholic, he hath recommended and doth recommend his soul unto God the Creator, unto the Savior and Redeemer Jesus Christ, unto the glorious and very sacred Virgin Mary, unto Monsieur Saint Michael, angel and archangel, unto Messieurs Saint Peter and Saint Paul, and unto all the blessed saints of Paradise, supplicating them very humbly to be his intercessors and pray God for him, now and when his soul departeth from his body, that He may be pleased to receive it in His Paradise. . . . Item, he wishes and orders that his body be buried and interred in the parish church of the place where he shall die, and as to the funeral procession, lights, services, and funeral expenses, the said testator leaves this to the discretion of his executors afore-

said, or one of them." As he died in Tours, he is buried there in the choir of St. Martin's Church.

Those are without doubt the words of a devoted son of the Mother Church; and nine years before, Gourgues had fought on the Catholic side at the siege of La Rochelle. The Florida episode in his life is therefore "all the more worthy of admiration," says Samaran, "for it denotes in him an impartiality, a high-minded point of view rather rare at that time."

The will calls attention to several other points of interest. Dupleix says that Gourgues never married, but he did not tell the fact that the captain left a natural daughter, Claude, whom he made his sole legatee, and who must have been very young in 1581, since he stipulates that after his death she was to be put in possession, or her guardians "if then she be not yet of age and enjoying her rights," of the house and property known as Le Baqueraillon, two kilometers northeast of Mont-de-Marsan, which can be seen and visited to this day.

Gourgues made his lifelong friend, Pierre de Vaquieux, one of the two executors of his will. Vaquieux was Collector of the villain-tax for Condomois,[26] a little district—"un petit pays," as the French say—not far from Mont-de-Marsan. Dupleix writes that he was in the employ of Ogier de Gourgues, who was "a very opulent, splendid, and magnificent man, whose house and purse were open to all persons of merit. The captain, never having married, was cherished by him as a brother and a son, and by his order and with his means Vaquieux furnished him with all he needed for his voyage" to Florida.[27] There is a strong likelihood that during the year 1570, when Dominique was in hiding in Paris, he had ample leisure to relate to Vaquieux all the incidents of his extraordinary expedition to the east coast of Florida, and that the dramatic and picturesque narrative, "La Reprinse de la Floride par le Capitaine Gourgues," with its delicately flavored French wit and irony, is due either to the pen of Pierre de Vaquieux or to that of Gourgues himself. Writers disagree on this subject; some incline to Gourgues as being the author, others to Vaquieux.

Although Mont-de-Marsan, Gourgues' home town, has not yet set up a monument to his memory, as Maurice Delpeuch, his great admirer, suggested should be done, he is not entirely forgotten in the region. A street of Mont-de-Marsan bears his name; there is a portrait at the hôtel de ville supposed to be of him (but Samaran proves it to be that of his nephew); and there is a spirited old song in Gascon verse, called "Menicoun de Gourgues," which was sung a few years since at a local celebration by a native of the Department of the Landes, Abbé Dauge.[28]

"Dominique having sold, it is said, most of his property," wrote in 1861, the Viscount Alexis de Gourgues, one of his descendants, "he lived with his brother Ogier; and a few years ago, at the Chateau de Vayres, there was still left a souvenir of this. There were at the angles of the lawn, which is in front of the terrace, four very old green trees; I have only seen two of them, and the tradition was that Dominique had brought back [from Florida] those trees of a then unknown species, and he planted them on his brother's place."[29]

Basanier's abridged version of Gourgues' Florida epic is known in English through Richard Hakluyt's translation in *A Notable Historie,* but the original and remarkable longer chronicle, "La Reprinse de la Floride," has never been translated until now. It has been a great pleasure to do it, so that the dashing hero of old Gascony, the clever, unselfish Cyrano of the sixteenth century may become even better known than he is already. The avenging of France's wrong was his inspiration, his ideal, his *panache,* for, says Father Daniel, "according to the genius of his country, he loved glory more than any other thing." [30]

NOTES

1. The Viscount's article is "Dominique de Gourgues," in the *Bulletin du Comité de la Province Ecclésiastique d'Auch,* II (1861), 466-90.

2. "Un glorieux épisode maritime et colonial des guerres de religion: Le Capitaine de la marine royale Dominique de Gourgues et le massacre de la colonie protestante de la Floride (1565-1568)," *La Revue Maritime,* 1902, pp. 1882-1931, 2150-91.

3. *Histoire de la Marine française* (Paris, 1899-1932), IV, 46-70.

4. Charles Samaran, "Dominique de Gourgues," *Revue Historique,* CVIII (November-December, 1911), 276-93.

5. "Al fin persuaderon, y aiudaron con secreto a Domingo Gurgio (hereje terrible), a que pasase a vengar el agravio hecho a su maldita secta, en la justicia de Ribas y sus compañeros. . . ." *Ensayo cronológico,* Year 1507, p. 133.

6. For copies of papers relating to the sale of the artillery, see the Appendix to Tamizey de Larroque's version of "La Reprinse de la Floride" (Paris, 1867), pp. 71-76.

7. *Histoire de la Floride française* (Paris, 1875), p. 319.

8. ". . . n'eust esté que monsieur de Chastillon, avec sa façon sévère et pleine de gravité, remonstra que si Gourgues avoit eu tant de courage que d'entreprendre luy seul ce que toute la France devoit faire, il méritoit une grande récompense et non pas une punition, et que ceux qui le condamnoient d'un acte si généreux sembloient desjá nous vouloir honteusement assuiettir au vasselage de notre ennemi capital; si bien que mesme le roy Charles neuvième, qui estoit courageux et surtout esmeu en la ieunesse où il estoit; et vous no sçauriez croire combien l'arrest qui s'en suivit apporta de gloire et d'honneur à l'amiral, voire mesme par la bouche des ambassadeurs estrangers qui estoient à la cour." *La Fortune de la Cour,* p. 242.

9. "Il fut si bien défendu par les principaux de la cour et singulièrement par l'amiral, que Sa Majesté et son conseil jugèrent qu'en vengeant ses injures particulières, il avait aussi vengé celles de la France." Dupleix, *Histoire de la France* (Paris, 1658), III, 674.

10. MS Fr 20794, pp. 736-37.

11. "Un glorieux épisode," pp. 2181, 2183.

12. Saulx-Tavannes, *Mémoires,* S.24: "Les courtisans esbahis iuroient que le roi deviendroit huguenot."

13. Samaran, "Dominique de Gourgues," p. 278.

14. Gaffarel, *La Floride française,* pp. 326-27.

15. Delpeuch, "Un glorieux épisode," p. 2182.

16. " . . . du crédit, confiance, suffisance, vaillance, expérience, capacité, bonne conduite et diligence du capitaine Gourgues." Delpeuch, "Un glorieux épisode," pp. 2182, 2183.

17. Royal letters which sanction the execution of a decree.

18. Delpeuch, "Un glorieux épisode," p. 2184.

19. La Roncière, *La Marine française,* IV, 123-24, 132-33.

20. Philip II to Guzman de Silva, March 2, 1566, in Martin Hume (ed.), *Calendar of Letters and State Papers, Spanish, 1558-1567* (London, 1892), I, 536.

21. La Roncière, *La Marine française,* IV, 137.

22. Delpeuch "Un glorieux épisode," p. 2187.

23. "M. de La Garde m'a envoyé à dire présentement qu'il doit arriver à nuyt dix-sept navires de guerre d'Angleterre pour entrer dans La Rochelle; et m'a commandé, souldain que les verre, me mettre à la voille et m'en aller à Brouaige, ce que je ne veulx faire. L'honneur nous commande de n'abandonner si paoureusement la rade; et qu'il vous plaist commander aux autres deux navyres (l'Anjou et le Henry) de se tenir auprès de moy et leur bailler des soldats, nous les combattrons et empescherons, si les gallères veullent faire leur debvoir, qu'ils n'y entrent pas." La Roncière, *La Marine française,* IV, 141; *Archives Historiques de la Gironde,* X, 371.

24. La Roncière, *La Marine Française,* IV, 153.

25. A copy of it exists in the Archives Nationales, Paris, 123, fol. 415.

26. "Receveur des tailles du Condomois."

27. *Histoire de France,* III, 675.

28. Samaran, "Dominique de Gourgues," p. 276.

29. "Dominique de Gourgues," p. 490; Delpeuch, "Un glorieux épisode," p. 2190.

30. Le Père Gabriel Daniel, *Histoire de France* (Paris, 1729), VIII, 595: "Suivant le génie de son pays, il aimoit la gloire plus que tout autre chose."

The Recapture of Florida

mong many strange things unknown in past centuries which *God* has reserved for the men of this time, the most admirable to my mind is a fourth part of the earth discovered eighty years ago, as large or larger than the three already known and described by the ancients; and an infinite number of beautiful islands around this new land, from which an infinite number of helpful things have come to us: this among others (which studious men will not esteem the least) that geography, hitherto lacking half of itself, has by this means now achieved its completion and perfection: and the natural history of animals, plants, precious stones, and metals has thereby been greatly augmented. The existence of many good things which the ancients had rather inferred by reasoning than known by experience was thereby confirmed: such as, that there are people there; and (what one might hardly have dared to hope) that one can go there and return from there; negotiate, trade, and make contracts with the natives there. Many deep-rooted errors were thereby corrected: such as, that

the earth between the two tropics was uninhabitable, barren, and burned: whereas it has been found to be densely populated, and more fertile and temperate than it is even in the regions which hitherto have had the name and reputation of being so.

This discovery having been made by Christopher Columbus, a Genoese, in the year one thousand four hundred and ninety-two, the Kings of Spain and Portugal, who are the nearest thereto, and who were the first advised thereof, sent at once, each on his own account, to take possession of this land, as much as they could, in order to be alone, or the first, to enjoy the great riches that had been reported to them, which have since surpassed their expectation and that of all men. But this land being so large, as we have said, all they could do was to traverse a large part thereof and discover the best places to stop at and settle. And after having occupied as much of it as they could, there still remained more of the country than all the princes of Europe could hold. In this empty land, unoccupied by them, was Florida. At the beginning of the reign of King Charles IX, who is reigning at present, the French went there, took possession thereof for the King, and erected two stone columns with the coat of arms of his Majesty. And having built a fort there, on the River of May near the sea, and accommodated themselves with houses for the number of them there were, they were in command there, with the consent of the Indians, until the year one thousand five hundred and sixty-five,[1] when the Spaniards, jealous of the fact that the French wanted a share of this new world, resolved to execute on them by treachery that which they could not hope to do as honest men. And under color of the peace and alliance which existed between the most Christian and Catholic Kings, they made a descent on the coast of Florida with a great number of vessels in the month of September, 1565, and asked if they might speak to Captain Jean Ribault, the King's lieutenant, who had lately arrived in that land of Florida with a commission and with powers from his Majesty. Ribault came to them in good faith, and with all his company was cruelly and treacherously massacred by them. Then these traitors and murderers hastened to find the other Frenchmen who lived around the fort in a small number, not suspecting any treachery, and killed them, and entered and took possession of the fort.[2] And when they found no more men, threw themselves on the poor women, and after having by force and violence assaulted most of them, they struck them all down and cut the throats of the little children without mercy. Now it must be noted that when they saw they had the upper hand of the French, they took as many of them alive as they could, and having kept them three days without giving them anything to eat, and having made them endure all the torments they could devise, they hanged them on trees which were near the fort. They even flayed the King's lieutenant, and sent his skin to the King of Spain. They tore out the eyes of those they had murdered, and having stuck them on the ends of their daggers, competed among themselves to see who could flick them the farthest.

The news of this cruel massacre having been brought to France, the French people were wonderfully incensed at such cowardly treachery and detestable cruelty; and particulary so when they heard that the traitors and murderers, instead of being blamed and punished in Spain, were praised there, and rewarded by receiving the greatest estates and honors. All Frenchmen expected that such a wrong done to the King and the whole French nation would be soon avenged by public authority, but as they were disappointed in that expectation for the space of three years, they hoped that some private citizen might be found who would undertake to perform an act so glorious in itself and so necessary to the honor and reputation of France. Some men *there were who would not have been loath to receive the praise due the accomplishment of such an enterprise; but there were so many difficulties, and such great ones, that the bitterness of these offset the glories. The thing could not be done without great expense, in construction and equipment of the ships, in arms and munitions, and in food and salaries of the soldiers and sailors who were needed. Few people could, still less would, make such an expenditure. Furthermore, the undertaking, for many considerations, was very uncertain, hazardous, and perilous, and what is worse, one could not see how this enterprise, even were it conducted and executed wisely and successfully, could be exempt from dangerous controversy. It was therefore very difficult to find a person who would overcome that dangerous controversy together with the loss of his property and with an infinity of other perils and inconveniences. Captain Gourgues, however, a Gascon gentleman of the Viscounty of Marsan, inspired by the zeal he has always shown in the service of his King (wherein he has been continually employed since his youth, in Scotland, Piedmont, and Italy as well as in France, according to whether his Majesty's affairs presented themselves on sea or on land), closing his eyes to all these difficulties which he well foresaw, undertook to carry out this revenge which was so just or to die in the attempt.*

Captain Gourgues, therefore, at the beginning of the year 1567, seeing that his services were not required in Europe, the kingdom being at peace within and without and there being no indication yet of the civil wars which broke out afresh nine months afterwards,[3] resolved to go to Florida to see if he could avenge the insult done to the King and to all France. And although he began to make his preparations at the beginning of the year, he was not ready to sail before the month of August. It was an undertaking which required not only ability and experience, but, as we have said, it needed a great expenditure, for which the income of a mere gentleman could not be sufficient; and his was less than that of others because all his life he had applied himself more to acquiring honor and reputation than to amassing a fortune. So that finding himself short on that side he sold his property and borrowed from his friends enough to build, arm, and equip two small vessels shaped like a roberge,[4] and a patache after the manner of a Levantine frigate which, lacking wind, might be propelled by oars and be fit to enter the mouth of the large rivers;[5] also enough to buy one year's supplies and other necessary things for the soldiers and sailors he intended to take. Having done all these things and having seen well to all matters, he embarked at Bordeaux the second day of August, with the permission of Monsieur de Montluc, lieutenant for the King in Guyenne. Yet his leave of absence did not mention going to Florida, but going to the coast of Benin, in Africa, to make war on the Negroes. He descended the river to Royan, twenty leagues from Bordeaux, where he passed the muster of his men, soldiers as well as sailors. There were one hundred arquebusiers, many of whom were gentlemen, all having arquebuses of the regulation calibre, with morions on their heads; and eighty sailors who, if need be, knew well how to perform the duty of soldiers. He had suitable arms for them, such as crossbows, pikes, and all kinds of long, wooden-handled weapons. After calling the muster roll, Captain Gourgues gave out the place of meeting, as is the custom on such expeditions. But as he was about to depart, a contrary wind arose which compelled him to remain eight days at Royan. That wind having abated a little, he put out to sea and set sail. Soon afterwards he was driven back towards La Rochelle and not even being able, on account of the violence of the weather, to stay in the harbor of La Rochelle, he was compelled to retire to the mouth of the Charente and remain there eight days. Because of these events he was much distressed on account of the supplies being consumed, and because of the fear he had that his men might take that delay for an ill omen, and lose the high spirits they had shown since the beginning.

The twenty-second day of August, the wind having ceased, and the sky showing signs of milder weather for the future, he again put out to sea and set sail. The weather was hardly auspicious to him. With great difficulty he reached the Cape of Finibus-Terrae[6] where he was once more assailed by the west wind, which blew for the space of eight days, during which he was in great danger of shipwreck. He had great trouble with his men, who prayed to him earnestly to return. The vessel which had his lieutenant on board strayed away, and for fifteen days it could not be known whether she was safe or lost. She finally reached the meeting-place, which was at the Lor River in Africa, where Captain Gourgues was awaiting her. Here he allowed his men to rest and refresh themselves. They were so weary and overworked that they were worn out. He consoled and conforted them by all the means he could think of, and when he had well reassured them and restored their health, he had the anchors hoisted. Coasting along part of Africa he reconnoitered the countryside as he passed, in order the better to be able to serve his Majesty there, if the opportunity were to present itself. While he was sojourning at Cape Blanco (to accustom his men to the climate and by this means keep them in health) three Negro kings came to attack them, instigated by the Portuguese who have a castle called Arguil five leagues from there, and who did

205

not dare come themselves. These Negroes were twice so vigorously received that they would not go back a third time, and abandoned the harbor to Captain Gourgues. However, he departed from there soon after, and again sailing along the coast of Africa, reached Cape Verde. From thence he took the course to the Indies, sailing on the high seas.

Having crossed the Northern sea, the first land he touched was an island called Dominica, inhabited by savages only, where he remained eight days on account of the good water to be found there. Then pursuing his way he came to another island called San Germán of Puerto Rico, which the Spaniards hold. Here they found a kind of fig, very large and long, which grows on bushes. It is green and prickly outside and red as scarlet inside. They ate some on the advice of one who had been to Florida at the time the French ruled there, whom the Captain brought with him to serve him as a trumpeter and an interpreter. The figs are a little bitter, yet have a very good taste, and greatly satisfy thirst. But when one has eaten half a dozen, they make one urinate freely, and render the water as red as the color of their insides. Our men thought they were passing blood and dying, and cried out against the trumpeter who laughed at them. When they were about to rush upon him, he assured them that there was no danger, and that it was the nature of this fruit so to color urine without doing any harm.

Departing thence, they arrived at Mona Island, inhabited by savages only, very fertile and luxuriant, where among other fruits are found the best and most beautiful oranges, lemons, and melons ever yet eaten, and a sort of fig half a foot long, of the shape of a cucumber, having a green skin and a yellow inside, very good to eat, which is called platane[7] in the language of the country. A species of root similar to turnips is likewise used there, which when cooked in water or over live coals has the taste of cooked chestnuts. The natives call it patate.[8] The inhabitants are good people and very simple. Their King came to see the ships of Captain Gourgues and spent two nights on board. Then he took the Captain on land to see his gardens, his house built in the manner of a cave, and his fountain, which he called Paradise, in the very deep hollow of a rock. One descended by steps to it, and he said that the water of that fountain was a cure for fevers. On Captain Gourgues' departing from this island, the King gave him a great quantity of fruit in return for some shirt linen Captain Gourgues had given him, since they do not have any over there.

Sailing thence, he coasted along terra firma towards Cape La Belle,[9] reconnoitering the country. Then contrary winds drove them back and threw them toward the island of Hispaniola, otherwise called Santo Domingo. It is today inhabited by Spaniards only, after they had put to death all the native Indians they found there, to the number of more than a million. The Spaniards either killed the natives by the knife, or by the continual labor forced on them in the gold and silver mines, without giving them any rest. By infinite kinds of ill treatment they constrained them to die by their own hands, or to poison themselves, or to let themselves perish of hunger without wanting to eat anything. And the poor Indian women were even reduced to forcing their offspring out of their loins before their time, in order to free their children by this means from Spanish slavery and from living a life worse than death. The thing is incredible if the Spaniards themselves had not exactly written all this in their histories. That is how they converted the Indians to the Christian faith they boast of. And yet those poor Indians were so docile before having experienced the cruelty of the Spaniards, when Christopher Columbus went there the first time, that they had only to see the Christians at prayer to kneel of their own accord, worship the cross, strike their breasts, and perform all the acts of devotion that they saw the Christians perform. They served these Spaniards with incredible promptness. Of this the Spaniards themselves give testimony in their histories.

So in that island, thus held by the Spaniards, Captain Gourgues was not even permitted to take on water, unless he did so by force. He found himself here in very great danger, the sea being horribly disturbed by a tempest and the land being still more his enemy, for the Spaniards are enraged as soon as they see a Frenchman in the Indies, although a hundred Spains could not furnish enough men to hold the hundredth part of a land so large and spacious. Nevertheless it is the opinion of the Spaniards that this new world was never created except for them, and that it does not befit a living man to walk or breathe in it except themselves alone. However, Captain Gourgues stopped here until the sea had subsided, being compelled to do so and assuring himself that he could more easily defend himself against Spaniards than against winds and tempests. Around this island and others near it are found tortoises so large that the flesh of one would suffice for more than sixty persons for one meal; and the shell could serve as a shield to the tallest man there is. The shell is so hard that a pistol would have much trouble piercing it. These tortoises remain in the sea during the day, and at night they feed on land, and lay their eggs in very great numbers in a hole in the sand. They are as good to eat as hen's eggs. Among others, one tortoise was caught, which, having four soldiers on her back, nevertheless did not stop moving ahead:

whereat I am not astonished, as I remember having read in Pliny, Book IX, Chapter 10 of his Natural History, that there are in the Indian Sea such large tortoises that the shell of one alone is sufficient to cover a house fit to live in, and that likewise in the other islands of the Red Sea they use them as skiffs. And in Book V, Chapter 22, that the tortoises of the Taprezane have such a large shell that it can cover an entire family of inhabitants.

The sea having become calm, Captain Gourgues departed from there and reached Cape St. Nicholas, which is on the same island of Hispaniola, where he had his ship caulked, which had been torn open by the storm, thereby causing him the loss of all the bread on board because it had been soaked. He almost lost everything else in the ship and the ship herself. But she arrived in good time at Cape St. Nicholas, where she was so well repaired that never thereafter did anything go amiss. This loss of the bread was an inestimable injury to Captain Gourgues and his company, for it became necessary to cut down the food by half, and he who previously ate two biscuits a day no longer took but one. In addition, the islands by which they had to pass later on were held by the Spaniards, such as the island of Cuba. This they found first after leaving Cape St. Nicholas. There the Spaniards would never give supplies in exchange for Rouen linen, or for other things that Captain Gourgues had brought for this purpose, in case his provisions gave out. They would not even allow them to take on water, but it was taken on in spite of them. Near this island the most violent and impetuous wind arose they had yet experienced, but it only lasted six hours. If it had been of longer duration, they would have been done for, as it would have thrown them on the coast where their vessels would have been lost, and they at the same time.

Cape St. Anthony is at the end of the island of Cuba, which they reached soon after the storm had abated. It is distant from Florida about two hundred leagues by sea. Here Captain Gourgues, having assembled all his men, declared to them what he had hitherto kept from them: How he had undertaken this voyage to go to Florida to avenge on the Spaniards the insult they had done the King and all France. He excused himself for not having communicated to them sooner the plan of his enterprise, showed them the means by which he hoped to succeed in his design, and prayed and exhorted them to follow up those means with as much heart as he had hoped from them, when he chose them from among many as the most fit for the execution of such a purpose. He lay before them the treachery and cruelty of those who had massacred the French, and the shame there was in having left so long unpunished such a wicked and un-

208

fortunate act. He showed them the honor which would redound to them for such a fine deed. In brief, he animated them so well that, although at the beginning they thought the thing well might be impossible (because of their small numbers and of that coast being one of the most dangerous in all the Indies), they promised nevertheless not to forsake him, and to die with him. The soldiers even became so ardent that they could hardly wait for the full moon to light their way through the Bahama Channel, which is very dangerous. The pilots and sailors who were cool at the beginning were soon warmed by that ardor of the soldiers. The moon therefore being full, they entered the Bahama Channel, and soon afterwards they discovered Florida.

When the Spaniards who were in the fort[10] saw the ships of Captain Gourgues, they saluted them with two cannon shots, believing them to be Spanish. Captain Gourgues, to maintain them in that opinion, replied in similar fashion, and pretending to go elsewhere, sailed beyond until night had come and he had lost sight of Florida. When night came, he turned sail and came down fifteen leagues from the fort, where the Spaniards could discover nothing, in front of a river which the savages call Jacatacourou, which the French have named the Seine River because it resembles our Seine.[11]

As soon as the day had dawned, Captain Gourgues, being in the road, saw the seashore all lined with savages armed with their bows and arrows to prevent him from landing, thinking he was a Spaniard. Captain Gourgues, who had well foreseen this, had also thought of the means of not being handicapped-- rather, helped--by them, and he therefore made all manner of signs of peace and friendship, and sent toward them his trumpeter who was well known to them and knew well how to speak their language, having talked with them when the French were there and built their fort. As soon as they recognized the trumpeter, they began to dance, which is an ordinary sign of joy among them, and asked him why he had so delayed in returning to them. He replied that it had not been his fault that he had not come sooner: "But I could not have come in safety," said he, "until now, for here are Frenchmen who have come hither to renew their friendship with you, and who bring you from France things that are the most necessary to you and that you like the best."

They began to dance harder than before; and their greatest King, called Saturiba, sent one of his men with the trumpeter to Captain Gourgues to bring him a roebuck and inquire further into the occasion of his coming. Captain Gourgues answered him who had been sent to him, that he should thank King Saturiba and assure him that what the trumpeter had said to

209

him was true; that they had only come there to associate themselves with him and the other Kings, and give them beautiful things made in France, which they lacked beyond the sea. He would not say more about his undertaking until he had seen that there was no Spaniard among them and had sounded the heart of the savages, and reflected on how everything was going. The savages, after having heard this reply, started to dance more than before. And a little afterward they sent back to Captain Gourgues to tell him they were going to notify all the Kings, relatives, and allies of King Saturiba to meet them in that place the next day, to associate themselves with the Frenchmen. In this they did not fail. So they departed for that day. Now, during all these goings and comings, Captain Gourgues had sent his pilot to take soundings in the entrance of the river, and had heard from him that it was navigable. Therefore he went up the river to be more under cover and to be able more easily to treat with the savages.

The next day the great King Saturiba came to the same place, and the Kings Tacatacourou, Halmacanit, Etore, Harpaha, Helinacape, Helycopyle, Mouloua, and others, all relatives and allies of King Saturiba. When they had come, they sent word to beg Captain Gourgues to land. This he did, accompanied by his soldiers carrying their arquebuses. When the Kings saw the French coming armed, they were somewhat frightened. They caused Captain Gourgues to be asked why he came to them armed, since they wanted to be associated with him. He replied that he saw them with their arms, and so he brought his. They at once commanded their subjects to lay down their bows and arrows, and had them taken away in large bundles and carried to their homes. Captain Gourgues had his men lay down their arquebuses and retain their swords, and thus he went to find King Saturiba, who came to meet him, and made him sit on his right hand on a wooden seat covered with moss, which he had ordered made similar to his own. When they two were seated, two of the most aged among them came to pull up the brambles and grass which were in front of them, and they all sat down on the ground in a circle.

As Captain Gourgues was about to speak, King Saturiba, who is not accustomed to the European customs, cut him off, telling him that since the Spaniards had captured the fort built by the French, Florida had never had one good day, that the Spaniards had continually made war upon them, had driven them from their houses, cut their maize, ravished their wives, carried away their daughters, and killed their little children; and although he and the other Kings had suffered all these ills on account of the friendship they had entered into with the French, by whom the land had first been inhabited, yet they had never ceased to love the French because of the good treatment they had received from them when they commanded there. He said that, after the massacre the Spaniards had perpetrated on the French, he had found a child who had fled to the woods, whom he had always nourished like his own child; that the Spaniards had done everything possible to get possession of him in order to kill him, but the Indians had always kept him to return him some day to the French, when they should come to Florida. "Since you are here," said he to Captain Gourgues, "take him, I give him back to you." Captain Gourgues, much pleased at finding the Indians so well disposed for the execution of his project, and that King Saturiba had even of his own accord entered first into the matter of the Spaniards, thanked him very affectionately for the good friendship he felt towards the French, and particularly for having saved that young man. He prayed them all to continue always that good affection, mentioning the greatness and goodness of the King of France. He said that, as to the Spaniards, the time was drawing near when they would be punished for the wrongs they had done and committed, as much against the Indians as against the French; and if the Kings and their subjects had been maltreated through hatred of the French, they would also be avenged even by the French.

"What?" said Saturiba, with a thrill of delight, "would you be willing to make war against the Spaniards?"

"And what do you think about it?" said Captain Gourgues, concealing his plan in order to bring it into play with proper effect. "It is time right now to avenge the insult they have done our nation; but for the present I had only intended to renew our friendship with you and to see how things are going in order afterwards to return at once against them, with such forces as I should see would be needed; yet when I hear of the great wrongs they have done and are doing you every day, I feel compassion for you, and a longing to fall upon them without any more waiting, to deliver you from their oppression today rather than tomorrow."

"Oh," said Saturiba, "what a great good you would be doing us! My, how happy we should be! All the others would be likewise."

"I think," said Captain Gourgues, "that you would willingly be of the party, and would not want the Frenchmen to have all the honor of having delivered you from the tyranny of the Spaniards."

"Yes," said Saturiba, "we and our subjects will go with you and will die with you." The other Kings made similar replies.

Captain Gourgues, who had found what he was seeking, praised and thanked them greatly, and in order to strike the iron while it was hot, he said to them: "Verily, if we wanted to make war, it would have to be at once. How much time would it take you to assemble your men ready to march?"

"In three days," said Saturiba, "we and our subjects could come here, to go with you."

"And meanwhile," said Captain Gourgues, "you will take good care that everything be kept secret, in order that the Spaniards may not have wind of it."

"Have no fear," said the Kings, "we wish them more harm than you do."

Captain Gourgues, seeing that the foundations of his enterprise were rather well and fortunately laid, thought he must not defer any longer giving to these good people what he wanted to give them; and he began to distribute among them what he had brought for this purpose, things whereof we make no account on this side because of the abundance of the material as well as the masters who know how to fashion it, and because we have always been accustomed to them. But they to whom these things are new, and who have neither the material nor the workmen to fashion it, esteem them infinitely, such as knives, daggers, hatchets, scissors, bodkins, needles, purses, mirrors, bells, rosaries of glass beads, and other similar things. And after having divided them among them all, according to the rank of each, as far as he could judge, he said to King Saturiba and the other Kings: "Think if there is anything else that you would like to have; do not be sparing."

They, although they were more than pleased with what they already had, yet seeing the good will of Captain Gourgues, answered that they would each very much like to have one of his shirts, for which they asked not to be clothed in them--unless it were sometimes on some notable occasion--but to have them buried with them after their death, as they do likewise with the most beautiful things they have been able to collect during their lives. Captain Gourgues immediately gave one to each of the Kings, adding to them besides all that was at hand that he thought could be agreeable to them. Then King Saturiba, who had two strands of silver beads around his neck, gave one to Captain Gourgues. The other Kings gave him deerskins dressed according to the fashion of the country.

While the savages were amusing themselves with their presents, Captain Gourgues (who thought of nothing but carrying out his enterprise and who would not lose one minute of time) questioned the young Frenchman whom King Saturiba had given him, and heard from him that the Spaniards might be

212

about four hundred in number, and how they had built two small forts at the mouth of the river of May besides the large fort which the French had erected on the same river, a league above. This young man, who was sixteen years of age, was a native of Havre de Grâce named Pierre de Bré, who, because of his knowledge of and proficiency in the two languages, was very useful to Captain Gourgues during that voyage, on returning from which he which he was restored to his parents.

Captain Gourgues, deliberating on sending to reconnoiter the forts, said to King Saturiba: "In three days, as you have told me, you will return here with your subjects. In the same time those I shall send to reconnoiter the enemy will also have returned, but in order to guide them one of your people is needed, a safe and faithful man." King Saturiba at once gave a nephew of his, called Olotoraca, a very valiant and loyal man, under whose leadership a gentleman from Comminges,[12] named Estampes, with two others, went to reconnoiter the forts. After Captain Gourgues had secured hostages from King Saturiba in exchange for those he was sending under the pledge of Saturiba's word--who were given to him as soon as asked for-- Saturiba said: "I will give you my only son,[13] and that one of my wives[14] whom I love the most, so that you may know

that we are not liars nor traitors, as are these Spaniards who deceive us always, and never do anything of what they promise us."

Captain Gourgues was much pleased that his affairs were progressing, and in order to send off the savages, that they might the sooner be back, he said to them: "They have done you much harm, those wicked men, but this time we shall get the upper hand of them. To the end that we may the more easily capture them, I pray you not to delay longer than the three days you have asked for, and to keep the undertaking very secret"; which King Saturiba and the others promised to do; whereupon they went home dancing and leaping for joy, and Captain Gourgues retired to his ships with his hostages. The King's son was entirely naked, as were also all the other men. The King's wife was clothed in moss, and was about eighteen. They remained three days on board Captain Gourgues' vessels, awaiting the return of those who had gone to reconnoiter the fort. Three days from that time, at nearly the same hour, on one side appeared the gentleman from Comminges, who made his report of what he had seen, and on the other, the Kings with a goodly number of their subjects, well armed with bows and arrows, ready to march.

Here, before departing, the savages brewed a certain

beverage called by them cassine, which they are accustomed to drink when they go to fight in a place where there is danger. The beverage, made from a certain herb and drunk very hot, preserves them from hunger and thirst for the space of twenty-four hours. They presented some of it first to Captain Gourgues, who pretended to drink of it, but did not swallow any thereof. Then King Saturiba took some, and after him all the others, each according to his rank. That done, with many ceremonies, they all raised their hand, and swore and promised that they would do their duty of fighting well, and would not forsake Captain Gourgues.

Before all this had been accomplished, most of the day had gone by. Nevertheless they did not alter their plan of departing that very day, and the savages said they could journey all night, praying Captain Gourgues to have them taken across the river of Tacatacourou in his ships, for the place where were the Spaniards lay on the other side of the river. Captain Gourgues, seeing them thus resolved, assigned them a place where they were all to meet (as well as he could judge from the report made to him), which was at the mouth of a river, named by them Halimacany and by the French who had inhabited the country called the Seine.[15] Then he had them taken across the river, except Olotoraca. As his bow had not been brought

back to him since he had departed from the village with the others, he asked for arms, and then a pike was given him, wherewith he knew well how to help himself against the Spaniards. When the savages had crossed the river, Captain Gourgues began to exhort his men, pointing out to them the good frame of mind of the savages and the ardor wherewith they were marching against the Spaniards, and relying on the fact that the Frenchmen would do much better, because their food, education, organization, and religion were better than those of these poor savages. When he wanted to continue, they all cried out: "Forward! forward!" as men who wished already to be in the fight, and who were all resolved to die in it if necessary. Then Captain Gourgues, with all his soldiers and sixty sailors, departed by sea in two barks he had, besides the three ships.

The care of the ships he left with the rest of the sailors under the command of Master François. He was a native of Bordeaux, captain and master of his vessel, and as experienced a man in matters nautical as there is in this time. He was charged to caulk them well all over and hold everything in readiness to return at the earliest date, if God gave them good success. "If God wishes," said Gourgues, "that I should die in such a just pursuit, I leave you everything I have here, and pray you to conduct and bring my soldiers back to France, as I trust you"; in saying which he gave François the keys of his chests and of everything he had there. This greatly moved the hearts of all, and likewise of the sailors who were remaining to guard the ships, who could not repress their tears.

The departure was full of sadness, and there is no man but would have felt his heart break at hearing so many farewells on one side and another, so many charges and recommendations from those who were going, to their relatives and friends, and as many other directions given in case they should not return. For on leaving their country they did not think they were going to Florida, as has been said. Yet amid all this you would have admired the cheerfulness of those people, who, although they thought they were going to an almost certain death, yet feared only that they might not arrive promptly enough for the deed of honor they hoped for.

When they reached the mouth of the river of Halimacany where the savages awaited them, which was about at break of day, the wind from the northeast began to blow so hard that they had a narrow escape from perishing. This occasioned such a delay that the savages could not cross the river that day. Captain Gourgues, however, crossed it with great difficulty, at about eight in the morning, and leaving there a boat of one of his vessels to help them over, made his journey by land to go and await them at the river of Sarauay,[16] which was four leagues from there.[17] But the trail was so bad and there were so many waters to be forded, so many woods to go through, that it took them from eight in the morning to five in the evening to make those four leagues, Captain Gourgues always carrying his cuirass on his back: and they found nothing to eat all day, except a few roots of wild palmettos, wherefore they were so weary and famished that they were exhausted. When they reached the river of Sarauay, they found there three Kings of savages waiting for them, each leading one hundred men.

Now, from that river of Sarauay to the first two forts, there might have been about two leagues. Captain Gourgues, who saw that the result of his plan depended on diligence and swiftness, although he had eaten nothing all day (because the sailors had not yet brought there the boat wherein he had had some of his supplies placed on leaving the river of Jacatacourou), nevertheless departed with ten of his arquebusiers and his guide to go to and reconnoiter the first fort, in order to attack it the next day in the morning. The way across country was as difficult and troublesome as what had gone before. The night was dark and obscure. A little river which is quite near the fort was high because the tide was beginning to rise, and it could not be passed, so Captain Gourgues was compelled to return to his men at the river of Sarauay, wearied by the journey and angered at having done nothing. One of the Kings, named Hilicopile, seeing him come back very thoughtful, asked the interpreter in his language: "What ails thy King?" The interpreter answered him that he was grieved because he had not been able to reconnoiter the fort. "Tell him," said Hilicopile, "that I will lead him along the seashore without finding any mud or marshes, but the way thereby is longer." Captain Gourgues, hearing this, wanted the King to start at once. Accompanied by King Hilicopile, he departed with all his men, and sent two other Kings through the woods to be next morning at the ford of the little river which they had been unable to cross, quite near the first fort. He made his men hasten and marched with great diligence to be there at daybreak before he could be seen.

As the day began to dawn, he arrived at that river which was high and swollen by the risen tide. Nevertheless he had the ford sounded by one of his sailors, who found it could not be passed, whereat he was greatly vexed, for he had arrived just in time to surprise the Spaniards, who were still asleep. He decided to retire into the wood adjoining the river, to await the ebbing of the tide and then go and attack them at once. He was scarcely in the wood before it began to rain so hard that the drops trickled from all the trees over them, and the soldiers had much trouble to keep their fire. Daylight having come, Captain Gourgues could see the fort at his ease from the place where he was, and having looked well on one side and another and reconnoitered the whole, he noticed that there was only the beginning of a moat, and was therefore confirmed in the resolve he had made on entering the wood, to attack the fort as soon as he could pass the river. Meanwhile he saw the Spaniards working in the fort, which caused him to have some doubt as to whether his coming was not discovered; but events proved that they suspected nothing, for after the capture of the fort it was seen that it was a well at which they had been working.

At about ten o'clock in the morning, the tide being low, he went to cross the river a little higher up, where between the river and the fort he had seen a small wood which would help him not to be seen, while he passed the river as well as while he was forming his men. As the water of the river came above the waist, he ordered the soldiers to fasten their ammunition to their morions, and take their arquebuses with their fuses in one hand, and their swords in the other.

At the crossing of the river there was such a great quantity of oysters that the soldiers' shoes were cut, and the feet of most of them were wounded thereby, for the oysters there are larger and their shells sharper than those that we usually see in Europe.

However, they were hardly across the river before they began to shoulder their arms again and prepare for the combat of their own accord. Captain Gourgues gave twenty soldiers to his lieutenant and ten sailors carrying fire-pots and fire-lances to set the door on fire, and he ranged his men in order of battle behind the little wood where they could not be seen. He knew that no great exhortation was necessary as he observed them to be confident and well inclined. Moreover, the point he had reached required prompt action rather than a long harangue, and so he made it short. "I can well see, my friends", said he, "that your heart grows with the need, and I chose you for being men of such mettle. Your assured countenance predicts to me that we shall avenge today the insult done to our King and to France, our country." And pointing to the fort, whereof they could catch a glimpse through the trees: "There," said he, "are the thieves who have stolen this land from our King; there are the murderers who have massacred our Frenchmen. Forward! Forward! Let us avenge our King, avenge France, show ourselves Frenchmen!" And immediately he commanded his lieutenant to go against the door with his company, and he with the remainder went against a very low terrace next to the fort, in the shape of a platform, where there was only the small beginning of a trench.

The Spaniards had just dined and were still picking their teeth when our men, with their heads down, taking great strides, were seen at two hundred paces from the fort, from a terrace by the gunner who had just mounted to that terrace, who at once began to cry out in Spanish: "To arms! To arms! Here are Frenchmen! Here are Frenchmen!" And immediately he discharged a big culverin which was on the terrace, and fired it twice. As he was about to load it a third time, Olotoraca, who had not been taught to keep his place in the ranks and was more swift in the running than any other, sprang forward and mounted the terrace, which was not very high, and transfixed him right through with his pike. The Spaniards, having rushed to arms at the cry of the gunner, sallied forth from the fort either to fight or to retire towards their comrades, according to what they should see when they were outside. Captain Gourgues, at their coming out, had arrived just in time at the foot of the platform, his lieutenant being near the door. As he was mounting the platform, his lieutenant called out that the Spaniards were escaping, and then Captain Gourgues, returning quickly toward the door, shut them in between his lieutenant and himself, so that out of sixty there not one escaped death. By order of Captain Gourgues they took as many alive as they could to do to them what they had done to the French.

The first fort was no sooner taken than they went to attack

217

the second, which was on the other side of the river of May, opposite the first, that they might succor each other. It continually fired great cannon shots while the first fort was being captured, and greatly inconvenienced our men. The French turned against the second fort three artillery pieces they had found in the first fort, and also the culverin found on the platform, which was marked all along with the coat of arms of the late King Henry, whereat they knew that it had been taken from the French at the time of the massacre. This fact irritated our Frenchmen still more; and with these four pieces they continued to fire against the second fort, while Captain Gourgues with eighty arquebusiers quickly crossed the river in the boat that had been brought there just in time.

He landed between the fort and a wood there was very near it, suspecting what would happen, that the Spaniards would flee into the woods to retreat afterwards into the large fort, which was one league from there. Captain Gourgues was hardly across the river when the savages, who could not wait for the boat to be returned for them, leaped into the water, and swimming with one arm and holding their bows aloft with the other, they covered all the river from bank to bank.

The Spaniards to the number of sixty, seeing such a great and resolute multitude, and not distinguishing between the French and the savages because of the surprise that seized them, and thinking they could escape into the woods, precipitated themselves among the Frenchmen there who discharged their arms on them so thick and fast that most of them fell dead, stretched out on the spot. The others, wishing to turn back, found themselves surrounded by the savages. Thus, not being able either to fight or to flee, they threw down their arms and begged for life, which was taken from them as they pled for it.

Captain Gourgues succeeded with great difficulty in having fifteen kept alive, that the same might be done to them as they had done to the French. After they had been sent away, Captain Gourgues entered the second fort, from which he had everything at once removed that he had found there. Then he recrossed the river with his prisoners, and returned to the first fort so as to fortify himself there, not knowing what courage the others would have, nor how long it would take him to subdue the large fort, which was one league thence on the same river, on the side where the second fort was. Among the prisoners he held was a sergeant of a band, an old soldier from whom he learned the height of the large fort's walls, and the place whereat he could most easily capture it.

Those first two forts were taken on the eve of Low Sunday, 1568. Captain Gourgues remained Sunday and Monday.

Meantime he had eight ladders made of the height which had been shown him in a plan of the whole fort, which work the old soldier understood well. He had, besides, so well provided for the undertaking that the whole country was raised in arms against the Spaniards, so that those in the big fort dared not come out to look around. However, they disguised a Spaniard as a savage, and sent him on Monday to reconnoiter what people the French were and how many there were of them. Captain Gourgues was in the neighborhood of the fort with Olotoraca, his constant companion. The Indian recognized the Spanish spy, who was immediately seized. At the beginning he tried to use cunning, saying that he was one of the soldiers guarding the first fort, who, not having been able to retreat to the large fort because of the multitude of the savages, had thus disguised himself for fear of being killed by them, and that he had preferred to give himself up to the mercy of the French rather than put himself in danger of being massacred by the savages. But when the sergeant of the band, who was at once sent for, had asserted to him that he was one of the garrison of the large fort, and a spy, he confessed that he had been sent by the governor of the large fort to learn who was this newcomer and how many men he had. Captain Gourgues inquired of him how those at the large fort estimated the French forces. He replied

that the Governor had been given to understand that he had two thousand Frenchmen, whereat the Governor and his men, to the number of two hundred and sixty, were so astonished that they knew not what they were doing.

Captain Gourgues was well pleased at this news, and deliberated on going to attack them the next day while they were in that state of fear. In fact, that very day he made all his preparations, and gave his orders as to those he was going to leave to guard the mouth of the river and the fort there. This he left in charge of Captain Mesmes, his ensign, with fifteen arquebusiers. When night had come, he caused the savages to depart and to lie in ambush in the woods on both sides of the river. The next morning he left with his men, taking with him the band sergeant and the spy bound together, that they might show him in reality that which they had told him in words and by description. On the way, Olotoraca, King Saturiba's nephew (the one who had killed the runner at the first fort), a courageous and marvelously valiant man, said to Captain Gourgues, whom he never left, that he had served him well up to then, fulfilling all promises, but that he knew he would die at the capture of the large fort. He said for the mere sake of life he would not want to fail to be there; "and I pray you," he said, "to give to my wife what you would give me if I had lived, that she may bury it with me, and I may be the more welcome when I reach the village of souls.'' Captain Gourgues said that he would rather recompense and honor him alive than dead, and hoped to bring him back alive and victorious.

Meanwhile they discovered the fort, and as soon as the Spaniards saw them they began to fire on them from two double culverins which were on a bulwark that commanded all along the river. Captain Gourgues quickly reached a mountain covered with woods and forests at the foot of which was the fort. The high land extended from the place where he had been seen to a point very far beyond the fort. By means of the trees which concealed him, he drew as near to the fort as he could without being detected or molested. He halted at a spot whence he could easily look into the fort. He had no intention to storm it that day, but decided to scale the walls the next morning on the side toward the mountain, where the moat was not flanked and where part of his men could fight those who would want to defend the rampart, while the others would mount. But it happened that the Spaniards made a sally with sixty arquebusiers to reconnoiter his forces. He saw them as they came out and went stealing along in the moat. He immediately ordered his lieutenant to go with twenty arquebusiers to the other side, to place himself between the fort and them. When he saw his lieutenant at a spot where he could prevent them from re-entering, he went straight towards them, commanding his men not to fire until they were quite near so that immediately after having fired they could put their hands to their swords. When the Spaniards were out of the moat, ready to climb the mountain, Captain Gourgues and his arquebusiers were at the foot and picked them out just in time at such close range that not a shot was lost. Many were slain on the spot, and the French, putting their hands to their swords, began to engage those who remained standing. As the Spaniards turned their backs to return to the fort, here came the lieutenant to charge them on the other side, so that there was not one Spaniard who had a way to re-enter the fort. They were all slain. Those within, seeing in a moment that they had lost all the best and finest of their men, and thinking that they who had caused that defeat were only a small part of a greater number, despaired of being able to hold out. Besides, they had no hope for any settlement with those whom they had so outrageously wronged, so they abandoned the fort, and fled into the woods which were on the other side of the fort. There Captain Gourgues had stationed a great multitude of savages who shot their arrows at the Spaniards. Among others, there was one who at one shot pierced the shield of a Spanish captain, and the arrow entered far into his body through the left nipple and knocked him down dead. Captain Gourgues, who had seen the Spaniards issuing forth, and had come running after them, stopped them between the woods and the fort as they were fleeing from the arrows of the savages, and there they were killed and cut to pieces, except those whom with great difficulty he was able to reserve for a robber's death.

In that large fort were found five double culverins, four minions, and other small iron pieces, with eighteen large barrels of powder. Plenty of arms were likewise found, such as arquebuses, corselets, shields, pikes, and other things. Next day, Captain Gourgues having had the artillery laden on two vessels, a savage who was cooking fish set fire to a train of powder which the Spaniards had made and no one had yet noticed. Fire caught in the powder, which overturned the magazines from top to bottom, and burned entirely the houses which were of pine wood. The men were not harmed because they were all outside, here and there, but everything within was burned and lost, so that Captain Gourgues brought nothing back from there except the artillery which he had already taken.

The Spaniards who had been taken alive in the last fort were led to the place where they had hanged the French. After Captain Gourgues had pointed out to them the injury they had done the King, massacring his subjects, robbing him of the land his Majesty had conquered and of the fort he had had erected, he said that they must have realized that such a cowardly treachery, such a detestable cruelty, exercised against a King so powerful and a nation so generous, would not remain unpunished. He said further that he, who was one of the least of the gentlemen the King had in his kingdom, had taken upon himself the avenging at his own cost and expense; and that if the most Christian and Catholic Kings had been enemies and at mortal war with each other, they could not, even so, have justified themselves for the treachery and extreme cruelty that had occurred. He reasoned that since their Majesties were friends and so closely allied, the Spaniards' deed could not but be considered abominable, and still less could a penalty be found corresponding to the deed.

"Although you cannot suffer the penalty you have deserved," said he, "it is necessary that you should endure that which the enemy can give you honestly, in order that others through your example may learn to keep the peace and alliance which you have so wickedly violated." That said, they were hanged to the same trees where they had hanged the Frenchmen, and instead of a placard Pedro Menéndez had had placed there, containing these words in the Spanish language: "I do this not as to Frenchmen but as to Lutherans," Captain

Gourgues had inscribed on a pine tablet with a hot iron: "I do this not as to Spaniards, nor as to Marannos,[18] but as to traitors, robbers, and murderers."[19]

The execution being thus accomplished, Captain Gourgues, who had done that for which he had undertaken the voyage, resolved to return. Not having enough men to leave in Florida to hold the forts, he decided to destroy them, for fear the Spaniards who occupied lands near there might again come and take possession and that this might even be an occasion to attract them there; or that the savages might fortify themselves therein. Access to occupied forts would be more difficult for the French King if it might please his Majesty to send some of his subjects to settle there later. It would be easier for them to build anew than to take the fortresses already built there, well enclosed and well supplied. In order that the savages should not take amiss the destruction of the forts--and so that they would approve by having represented to them how he had kept his word to them from the beginning and had avenged them on those who had tyrannized over them so cruelly, he took up the subject of destroying the forts, and used all the arguments that could serve him to persuade them that all he wanted to do was for their advantage and out of hatred for the wickedness and cruelty the Spaniards had shown there. To this the savages lent such a willing ear that Captain Gourgues had no sooner finished speaking than they ran straight to the fort, crying and calling to their subjects after them. There they worked so diligently that in less than a day they did not leave one stone standing on another.

After that, the French and Indians departed to return to the first two forts, which were pulled down with the same ardor as the first, and they hanged thirty Spanish prisoners who had been left there. One of these confessed to having hanged five Frenchmen with his own hand. He accused himself greatly, saying in his language that God is real and just; and that He had brought him at the end to the punishment with which He threatens those who are inhuman and cruel.

There remaining nothing more to do, Captain Gourgues returned to his ships which he had left at the mouth of the river of Tacatacourou, otherwise called the Seine, fifteen leagues from there. He sent his lieutenant, Captain Casenove by sea with artillery; and he went by land with eighty arquebusiers and forty sailors carrying pikes, keeping his men always in battle array ready for any adventures in the land of the savages, whom he did not trust very much. Wherever they went, they found the way filled with good people of the country. They came from all sides to meet him as their liberator, carryin cooked fish and other food for the soldiers. Among others came an old woman who said to them that now she would no longer regret to die, since she had seen the French once more in Florida.

When Captain Gourgues arrived at the river of Tacatacourou, where his sailors were with the vessels, he found that the master pilot had recaulked his ships, renewed the water supply, and prepared things so that all there was to do was to embark. Here therefore he took leave of the Kings, and admonished them to persist in the devotion they had always shown to the King of France, who would defend them against the Spaniards and against all others. And until his Majesty should send a goodly number of men for their protection and defense, they should hold themselves well on their guard and take care that they were not surprised. Those good people were the most grieved in the world, and they began to weep when they saw that Captain Gourgues wished to go and so did Olotoraca, who had fought better than he had prophesied about himself. But they were consoled at once when he told them that he would return twelve moons hence, and would bring them plenty of mirrors, hatchets, and knives, which are the things they like the best. They said they were going off to make their wives dance, which is the greatest sign of rejoicing they have among themselves.

After Captain Gourgues had taken leave of the Kings,

he had his men called together so that they might all render thanks to God for the victory He had given them, and pray Him to be their guide and conductor on their return to France. When they were assembled: "My friends," said he, "let us thank God for the good success He has given to our enterprise; it is He who preserved us from the danger of the storms at Cape Finibus-Terrae, at the island of Hispaniola, at the island of Cuba, and at the river of Halimacany; it is He who inclined the hearts of the savages to unite with us, it is He who blinded the judgment of the Spaniards in such a way that they could never discover our strength or realize their own. They were four to one in well-fortified strongholds, well provided with artillery, munitions, arms, and supplies. We, for all these things, had nothing with us but right, and yet we have vanquished them in less than no time. Therefore it is not to our strength that we owe victory, but to God alone. Let us thank Him then, my friends; acknowledge all our lives the great good He has done us; and pray Him to continue His favor towards us always, to guide us on our return and preserve us from all dangers. Let us pray Him likewise to be pleased to dispose the hearts of men in such a manner that the many dangers wherein we have placed ourselves and the many hardships we have endured, may find grace and favor before our King and before all

France; just as we have had no other end in view than the service of the King and the honor of our country.''

On a Monday, the third day of May, after having thanked and prayed God, the rendezvous was made as one is accustomed to do at sea, and the anchors being hoisted, they set sail with such a favorable wind that in seventeen days they covered eleven hundred leagues and finally arrived at La Rochelle on Monday, the sixth day of June, which was the very day of Pentecost. They were only thirty-four days on the return journey, yet such a great voyage did not take place without accident: for the patache was lost with eight men on board. Also the expedition had lost several gentlemen of substantial attainment and good family, bold and valiant as could be. They had fallen at the capture of the forts and the defeating of the Spaniards in Florida. Such were Anthoine de Péru, Bierre, Carault, and Bachue, who were Gascons, and Pons de Saint Onge, and a few soldiers, all of whom died fighting bravely after having performed the finest exploits and feats of prowess that one could have expected from noble and generous hearts, dedicated to the service of their prince and the honor of their country.

Besides the patache which was lost on the return voyage, the roberge captained by Deux went astray in the latitude of an island called Bermuda, and returned one month later than Captain Gourgues. Those who were on that vessel very nearly perished, first in the storm, then from hunger. For from the very time the Captain set sail they had, all of them, only enough food for twenty days, at the rate of one biscuit a day for each four of them. But God willed that Captain Gourgues, being five hundred leagues from France, met one d'Imbasque by name, a friend of his, who gave him ten quintals of biscuit, which did them an incredible good. This was all the more so because it took them almost less time to make the five hundred remaining leagues than it had taken to make all the rest.

Now, after Captain Gourgues had sojourned a few days at La Rochelle, where he received all honor, courtesy, and good treatment from the citizens, he set sail for Bordeaux, whence he traveled by post to go to Monsieur de Montluc, to render him an account of his voyage. He heard afterwards that the Spaniards were apprised of what had been done in Florida by some who saw him arrive at La Rochelle, and that the Spaniards had sent eighteen pataches with one roberge of two hundred tons to take him by surprise. They had arrived in the roadstead of La Rochelle the very day he had departed from there, and hearing that he had set sail, they followed him as far as Blaye. Had he been notified in time, nothing in the world would have made him refuse to deal with them. His response to their demand would have done justice to the situation.

Such in the main was the voyage to Florida of Captain Gourgues. In it one may observe a marvelous zeal in the service of the King and for the honor of France, a singular constancy and perseverance in spite of all obstacles, a great daring in all dangers, wisdom in management, and diligence in execution. Primarily to avenge the public wrong, which did not touch him anymore than any individual Frenchman, he sold his property and indebted himself, and made an incredible expenditure, and exposed himself to an infinity of dangers on sea as well as on land. When he was ready to go he was delayed by contrary winds for the space of three weeks, and consumed during that time many of his supplies. Having departed, he feared destruction by four different storms and tempests. In one he lost half his biscuit rations and was obliged to cut down the food by half; in spite of all obstacles, he was not stopped, nor did any danger take him by surprise. When he arrived in Florida, he shrewdly associated with the savages and well understood how to make use of them and thus to make up for the scarcity of men he brought. The diligence and swiftness with which he carried out his enterprise is greatly worthy of consideration; he was always watchful in his purpose, always in action, and never ceased until he had taken Florida and had killed those who had taken Florida from the French.

If the Spaniard has esteemed Pedro Menéndez worthy of being created Marquis and an Adelantado for having, at the expense of the public and with an infinite number of men, treacherously massacred a handful of Frenchmen against his given word and against the peace and alliance of the two Kings (that is, for having violated all rights divine and human and having put on Spain a perpetual mark of disloyalty and treachery), what shall we think of this Frenchman who, at his own cost and expense, with one hundred and fifty soldiers and eighty sailors, has reconquered Florida and killed the traitors, robbers, and murderers, has avenged the insult done to his prince and his country, and has by this means effaced the blot and stain which marred and dishonored the French name for having left such an injury so long unpunished?

The consequence and importance of the events were great for many reasons, but particularly because the new world (which is large and spacious enough to satisfy all the princes of Europe) furnishes a fine opportunity for his Majesty to exercise his power and to utilize the great means of doing good that God has given him. If he wishes to enlarge his domain and extend his rule, there is no place in the world richer, more extensive, or easier to conquer and hold than this is. If he wishes, by following the example and intention of his ancestors, to convert the idolaters to the Christian faith, there are millions of men there who do not know Our Lord Jesus Christ and who, because of their simple-mindedness will be easier to convert by Frenchmen, than those of the ancient times in the Holy Land. His Majesty could not undertake a more royal, more august enterprise than that of having the Christian faith implanted in those countries, having civilization and education brought to those poor, ignorant savages, giving them laws and establishing there a good society. Ten per cent of the men who died in the least of our civil wars would have been more than sufficient for conquering there an extent of territory equal to several kingdoms such as this one. There are so many poor people in such a large kingdom as ours, who having here neither house nor hut, could possess over yonder many leagues of land and gather in the produce of the many strange products which nature there plentifully brings forth. This kingdom would be diminished in nothing thereby, rather it would be unburdened. They would not change their King, but their fortunes. Where now because of their need they are useless subjects, they would become useful and profitable ones returning to France great riches and exquisite and precious things, this to the relief of all the French people, and to the great pleasure and contentment of his Majesty, whom may God be willing to maintain and increase in all grandeur and prosperity.

NOTES

1. This should be 1565.
2. It will be noticed that there is confusion in the order of events, for Ribault was killed at Matanzas Inlet after the capture of Fort Caroline on the St. Johns.
3. In 1568, after the breaking of the Peace of Amboise.
4. A heavily built boat, resembling a Dutch three-master.
5. The two small vessels were of 250 and 120 tons; the *patache*, of 50. Gaffarel, *Histoire de la Floride française*, pp. 268-69.
6. Cape Finisterre, on the coast of Galicia, in Spain.
7. Probably the banana.
8. *Patata* is the Spanish for potato. In French a sweet potato is called a *patate*.
9. There is no cape of that name. The writer probably meant Cape Isabella on the northern coast of the island of Hispaniola.
10. At St. Augustine.
11. The St. Marys River.
12. Comminges was an ancient division of Southern France, comprised in the present departments of Haute-Garonne, Ariège, and Gers.
13. Saturiba had more than one son.
14. The text says, "Those of my wives." In MS 19899 it is, "That one of my wives." What follows shows the latter to be correct.

15. This is a mistake, as the river of Tacatacourou was the Seine. In MS 19899 a river is mentioned at this point, called by the French the Somme.

16. Variants: Sarandy, Sarabay, Carabay.

17. If in the *Florida Grower's Atlas,* pp. 12 and 32, one studies the extreme northeastern coast of Florida, one realizes how easy it was to confuse the names of the rivers and creeks between the St. Marys and the St. Johns. The river of Sarabay was probably Fort George Inlet, for Velasco says, in speaking of the inlets immediately north of the río de San Mateo or river of May (the St. Johns): "The first of the most noted is, on passing the mouth of the river of San Mateo, that which is called *Carabay* [Sarabay], which is a very small bar, and therefore cannot serve except for shallops; two leagues farther on is another called *La Revuelta,* with two mouths on account of a little island it has at the entrance; and farther on two other leagues is the bar of Sena, where used to be the fort of San Pedro; this is a bar over which, if they await the tide, vessels of two hundred tons can enter." The bar of Sena being Cumberland Sound, La Revuelta is Nassau Sound, and Carabay, Fort George Inlet. Gourgues crossed two principal rivers before reaching the St. Johns, probably Nassau Sound and Fort George Inlet. The most difficult point to attempt to explain is that the Alimacani is mentioned first, after he leaves the Tacatacourou (the Seine or Sena or St. Marys), when we know that the land of Cacique Alimacani was Fort George Island, at the entrance of the St. Johns, and the river of that name cannot have been far distant. Le Moyne's map shows it as coming first, north of the St. Johns.

18 Converted Jews.

19. Historians differ as to the truth of any such execution by the Spaniards. Pedro Menéndez does not mention it, nor do his biographers Solís de Merás, Barrientos, and Mendoza; but Menéndez, with his hatred of the Lutherans, would have been capable of doing it.

The Appendixes

The Menéndez Will

n the name of God. Amen.--Be it known to all those who may see this last will and testament, how I, the Adelantado Pedro Menéndez de Avilés, Knight of the Order of Santiago, Adelantado of Florida and Captain-General of the Armada and galleons of his Majesty, being at present in this town of San Lúcar de Barrameda, sick in body but sound in mind, and possessed of my reason and good memory and full understanding, which God Our Lord saw fit to give me; and taking as I do for my advocate the glorious Virgin Saint Mary, the blessed Apostle Saint James, to whose Order I belong, that they may be my advocates and intercessors with my Lord Jesus Christ, that he may hold it well to save me; and believing as I do believe, truly and faithfully, in the mystery of the Most Holy Trinity, which is Father, Son and Holy Ghost, three persons and one only true God, in whom every faithful Christian must earnestly believe, and without it one cannot be saved; and wishing to put my soul in the clearest and straightest path

that I can to save it, and to leave my heirs in peace and concord, I make and ordain this my testament, in the following form and manner:

Firstly, I say and declare that being as I am in his Majesty's service in war, and having placed therein, as I have, the property which God has given me, and not having any thing certain which at present I can will; and Pedro del Castillo, a citizen of Cadiz, being as he is my relative and great friend, who has always succored and assisted me, that I might be able to maintain the affairs in my charge, especially in the conquest and settlement of Florida; and feeling as I do entire satisfaction with his Christianity and truth, I leave him as my testamentary executor, and give him full power in sufficient form in order that he can collect what his Majesty owes me, and can end and conclude any lawsuits and demands that may have been or might be brought; and if it shall be necessary to bring them again, he may be able to do so; and I likewise give him power so that he will be able to collect and shall collect all that may be due me or may appear due me, in whatever manner; and all the rest of the property I may or do hold in goods and chattels as well as in real estate, ships, licenses from his Majesty for galleons, pataches, shallops and zabras, and any merchandise whatever, which in any manner does or may belong to me; and as the said Pedro del Castillo shall collect them, he shall pay the debts I may appear to owe by written pledges, public instruments or in any other manner, and the said Pedro del Castillo shall likewise pay himself what I owe him, from the first of my said properties that he shall hold and collect; and when all my debts have been paid, from what shall remain he shall be able to buy and shall buy rents and properties wherever and however he deems best, and from what he so buys he may entail an estate in virtue of a Royal Cédula from his Majesty which I hold therefor, to which estate the said Pedro del Castillo may and shall attach the conditions and charges that may seem proper to him; which said estate, I the said Adelantado place henceforth in the name of Doña Catalina Menendez, my legitimate daughter, and the daugher of Doña María de Solís, my wife, in order that the said Doña Catalina may enjoy it for all the days of her life, and after her the eldest child that she may have, and in default of a male child, the eldest female child, always preferring the male to the female, even though he may be younger; but if she should have more than one male child, and the elder should not wish to be called by the name of Menéndez de Avilés, and the second son should be thus called, this latter shall have my said estate; and in case that the said Dona Catalina Menéndez, my daughter, shall have no son or daughter to inherit the said estate, it is my wish that after the life of the said Doña Catalina, it shall go to Pedro Menéndez de Avilés, my nephew, and the nephew of my said wife, the son of Alvar Sánchez de Avilés, my brother, and of Doña Berenguela de Valdés, his wife, and to his children and heirs with the same condition as above set forth and declared; and in case my said nephew shall not have children, either, then Doña María Menéndez, my daughter, the wife of Don Diego de Velasco, shall have and inherit the said estate, whom from then on I name to the said estate, and the children she may have, according to the form and order in this clause contained.

Item: I direct, and it is my will, that the said Catalina Menéndez de Avilés shall enjoy the gift that his Majesty made me of the provinces of Florida, with all the rents and appurtenances annexed and belonging to them, and the other distinctions, gifts and offices that his Majesty, by the asiento he made and commanded to be made with me relating to the discovery and settlement of Florida, has bestowed on me; except the twenty-five square leagues which his Majesty granted me in the said asiento, for which he will give me the title of Marquis; I wish, and it is my will, that after I shall be dead, and immediately thereupon, Doña María Menéndez y Avilés, my daughter, wife of the said Don Diego de Velasco, and her children, shall have and inherit this; and if she shall have no legitimate children to inherit it, it shall return to the family.

Item: I say that inasmuch as his Majesty commanded that an asiento and agreement be made with me on the conquest and settlement of Panuco, I directed that if Pedro Menéndez Marqués, my nephew, should wish to take the said conquest under his charge, and carry out the said asiento, he may do so, and from then on I donate it to him in accordance with the manner in which I hold it from his Majesty, in order that he may enjoy it all the days of his life, and after him the children he may have, under the condition that they must and shall be called by the surname of Menéndez de Avilés and not by others, under penalty of losing the right to have and enjoy it; and in case that the said Pedro Menéndez Marqués has no legitimate child, or that he should not be called by the said name and surname, as aforesaid, the said bequest and donation shall come to the person who shall inherit the said estate and entail, as aforesaid; and in case that the said Pedro Menéndez Mar-

qués should not want to take charge of the said conquest, as aforesaid, or should die before succeeding therein; in that case I name Pedro Menéndez de Avilés, my nephew, in order that he shall come into it instead of the said Pedro Menéndez Marqués, as has been declared; and in default of those above mentioned, it shall revert to my entailed estate.

Item: I direct that in what concerns my burial and masses and obsequies, I refer to the said Pedro del Castillo, that he may act in the way and manner that seems best to him and should be considered best; since in everything, likewise, I give him my full power aforesaid.

Item: I direct that to Doña Elvira Menéndez, my niece, the wife of Hernando de Miranda, 300 ducats be paid for the good offices she has done me.

Item: I direct that to Doña Maria de Pumar, a widow, who is in Florida in the company of my wife, another 300 ducats be paid, to aid in her marriage.

Item: I direct that to Doña Maria de Solis, the niece of my wife, 300 ducats be paid to aid in her marriage.

Item: I direct that to each of three sisters of Juan Quirós, my nieces, 200 ducats be paid, to aid in their marriage; the three who are marriageable.

Item: I say and declare that inasmuch as I have arranged

with the said *Pedro del Castillo*, to institute in *Avilés* a memorial for my soul, and for relatives and ancestors, I give said power to the said *Pedro del Castillo*, in order that he may buy the income-bearing property which seems to him suitable for the said memorial, in the form, quantity and manner which shall appear best to him; and I refer everything to the said *Pedro del Castillo*, and what he may do from henceforth I approve, and this my will being fulfilled, and what is contained therein being paid, I leave and establish as my lawful heir to the remainder of my possessions, rights and pending claims, the said *Doña Catalina Menéndez*, my legitimate daughter, and that of *Doña Maria Solis*, my wife, whom I establish as my residuary legatee; and I revoke and annul and hold as void and of no value or effect, all and whatever wills, bequests and codicils I may have made before this; I wish their notes and records to have no weight or value in or out of law; saving this one which I now make, which is my last and fixed will.

Item: I declare, and it is my wish, that the person who shall inherit my house and have my estate, in accordance with the form aforesaid, shall do so under the obligation and condition that having reached the age of twenty years, he must and shall reside, with his household and his wife, if he have one, in the province of *Florida* for the space of ten years; and in case a female should inherit my said entailed estate, in default of a male, it shall be with the same said obligation and condition that she and her husband are to reside the said time of ten years in the said Indies of *Florida*; because my aim, and zeal therefor, is to endeavor that *Florida* shall be settled in perpetuity, in order that the Holy Gospel shall be extended and implanted in those provinces; and it shall be understood that the woman who, in default of a male, shall inherit my estate, shall do so under the said obligation and condition, that being of the age of twenty, to twenty-five years at the furthest, she shall marry in order to be able to fulfil what has been said, to go and reside in the provinces of *Florida* with her husband; and if she should not do this, then the second named to my estate shall have it; and in case those named to the said estate should have no heirs, according to and in order aforesaid, from then on I summon to the said estate the nearest relative through father and mother, those of the father being preferred to those of the mother; and this same obligation and condition I place upon the person who shall inherit the property of *Panuco*, in accordance with that which is declared above.

Done in the town of *San Lucar de Barrameda*, on the 7th day of the month of January, in the year 1574, the witnesses present being *Pedro Delguera*, and *Pedro de Aguirre*, and Juan Perez, and Martín Suarez, Berlandino de Ureña, residing in this town, and his lordship, whom I, the said Notary Public, swear that I know; he signed it with his name in this register, and it is to be understood that the obligation of residing in Florida, as aforesaid, includes whoever may enjoy the twenty-five square leagues, with the title of Marquis.

Pedro Menéndez.

Before me, Luis de Leon, Notary Public.--And I, Luis de Leon, Notary Public of San Lúcar de Barrameda, for the Duke my lord and approved by his Royal Majesty, and by the gentlemen of his Royal Council, had this written and here affix my seal, and I am witness.

Luis de Leon, Notary Public.

This transcript of the said original will, from which it was taken, is truly and faithfully extracted, corrected and compared with the said original in the city of Cadiz, the 24th day of the month of January of the year 1575, the witnesses being Juan de Paredes, a Notary of his Majesty, and Juan de Rola, a citizen and resident of Cadiz.

The Codicil

In the name of God. Amen.- Be it known to all those who may see this will and what is therein contained, how I, Pedro Menéndez de Avilés, Adelantado of the provinces of Florida and Captain-General thereof, and of the Armada which sails in the Carrera of the Indies, and of that which is assembled at present in the harbor of the town of Santander; being sick in body of an illness that God Our Lord has seen fit to give me, although sound in my natural mind, which is such as His Divine Majesty was pleased to bestow on me; fearing death, which is a thing natural to every man; desiring to place my soul on the road to salvation; believing as I do, truly and firmly, like a Catholic Christian, in the Most Holy Trinity, Father, Son and Holy Ghost, three distinct persons and one only true God, and in all that which the Holy Mother Church of Rome holds and believes, and commands to be held and believed--agree to and acknowledge, make and ordain this my will and codicil, in the manner following:

Firstly, I commend my soul to God Our Lord and Savior Jesus Christ, and I pray His Divine Majesty when He may be pleased to take me from this life, by the merits of His Most Sacred Passion, and taking as I do for my mediator and advocate the Most Holy Virgin, Saint Mary, His Blessed Mother and Our Lady, that He may have mercy on my soul. Amen.

Item: I order that if, when the will of Jesus Christ, Our Savior and Redeemer, shall be pleased to take me from this present life, I should die in the town and port of Santander, where I am at present with the present Armada, being Captain-General thereof in the name of his Majesty the King Don Felipe, my master; or (if I should die) in any other place; my body shall be taken to the town of Avilés, and there interred in the Church of Saint Nicholas, where my ancestors are buried.

Item: I order that my executors shall expend for the repose of my soul, in masses and sacrifices in the Collegiate Church of the Holy Relics, of the town of Santander, and in the Monastery of Our Lady Saint Clara; and in the Church of Saint Nicholas of the town of Avilés, in masses and sacrifices for my soul and those of my ancestors; an amount of about 400 ducats in gold, which shall include the cost of the wax and the offerings that may be made, not only at the time of my funeral, but before and after; all in the order which may appear best to my executors; and of some mourning draperies if any be brought forth.

Item: I say and declare that before this my will, I made and executed another before a notary in the city of Cadiz, of whose name I have no recollection at present; which aforesaid will I left in the possession and in the house of Pedro del Castillo, a citizen of Cadiz; I say and order that the said will be opened, looked at and recovered, and that all that is contained therein be observed and fulfilled and executed with full force absolutely, because it so befits the service of God Our Lord and the relief of my conscience; and it is understood that this one which I make and execute at present by this my codicil, is and shall be an addition to what is known to be in the first will aforesaid.

Item: I say and delcare that I have held and do hold, by order of his Majesty, the office of Escribania Mayor of his Armadas, which I beseech his Majesty to order to be bestowed on the successor of my house and estate.

Item: I say and confess (that I owe) Señor Don Diego de Maldonado, my Lieutenant General of the present Armada, 2,500 silver reales, which he loaned me in Madrid; a little more or less, whatever he may say, because he is such a prominent gentleman that he will tell nothing save the truth. I order that this be paid to him from the most available funds, without any discount.

Item: I say and declare that in virtue of a draft of mine, Paymaster Fortuno de Ozaeta gave 1,000 silver reales to Alonso de Escobedo, Captain of one of his Majesty's zabras; I order that this shall be paid to the Paymaster aforesaid, and that the said Alonso de Escobedo shall render an account thereof.

Item: I say that it is already thirty-two years, more or less, since I have been serving his Majesty as Captain-General of his royal armadas, in which time I have spent many sums of maravedis, which I owe because his Majesty has not made me any gift to satisfy the said debts and to relieve my conscience.

I beseech his Majesty that, as he has promised me many times by word of mouth, he may do me the favor of granting me some financial aid wherewith my said debts can be satisfied; because in reality of truth, at present I have nothing to comfort my mind and soul; and this I beg of his Majesty with all the humility I can, and do owe to him, in recompense for so many hardships I have undergone and services I have done him, as well with the body as the mind, using always much loyalty and fidelity, such as I owe to the service of his Majesty.

Item: I order that an inventory be made of my clothing, arms, deeds and papers, and particularly of the letters and me-morials of his Majesty, which are in my possession; and that until his Majesty may order otherwise, they be placed and be displayed publicly and as an inventory, in the possession of Juan Menéndez de Recalde, a servant of his Majesty.

Item: I say and order that 200 gold ducats from the most available fund be given to each of my two nephews, Bartolomé de León and Quirós, who have served me very well as pages.

Item: I say and declare that in addition to what I beg that his Majesty may grant me as a favor, he owes me, and I charge him with many sums of maravedis, not only as my salary but likewise as moneys which I have spent in his service; I wish, and it is my will, that the heir aforesaid shall collect them; and I beseech his Majesty to order that they be paid to him, ordering that what is due me be ascertained.

In order to fulfill and pay for this my will, and the bequests and legacies contained therein, I appoint as my executors Señor Don Diego de Maldonado, Juan Menéndez de Recalde and Juan de Escalante, citizens and residents of the towns of Santander and Bilbao, and living at present in this town of Santander; Luis Gonzalez de Oviedo, a citizen of Oviedo, and Hernando de Miranda, my son-in-law, a citizen of Avilés.

Each and all and any one of whom in solidum, I empower and order to sell at auction, or otherwise, or by taking them, the most available articles among my property, that they may so fulfill this my will and the expression of my mind, according as I leave it declared.

And this having been so accomplished, I leave to my lawful heir, Doña Catalina Menéndez, my legitimate daughter, all the other goods and chattels and landed property, rights and pending claims to me belonging, in accordance with the tenor of what has been by me disposed of in the will aforesaid, which, thus made and executed, I give into the possession of the said Pedro del Castillo, a citizen of the aforesaid city of Cadiz; and I have here incorporated it as though it were here inserted word for word; and I revoke and annul and hold as void and of no value or effect, any other will or wills, codicil or codicils which previous to that above mentioned, and previous to this which I am making at present, I may have made and executed, either in writing or by word of mouth, in order that they shall be null and void, save the above mentioned, and this which I am making at present; all of which I wish to be valid as my will and codicil and as my last and final intention, in that manner and form which may legally best serve the purpose.

In proof and testimony of all that is said, I executed the present deed in the presence of Pedro de Ceballos, notary of his Majesty, of a number of persons of Santander and of the wit-nesses usually subscribed; whom I beg and pray to write and sign it in such manner that it shall certify that it was made and executed and read while I was in the house and place known as Hano, in the jurisdiction of the said town of Santander, on Wednesday, the 15th day of the month of September, in the 1574th year from the birth of Our Savior Jesus Christ; being present as witnesses to the aforesaid, and at the execution and reading of the said will, the said Señor Pedro Menéndez de Avilés, Fray Juan de Madariaga, Superior of the Monastery of San Francisco of Santander; Licentiate Martin Ruiz de Olalde, a physician, a citizen of the town of Portugalete; Gabriel de Untoria, the apothecary of the Armada, a citizen of the town of Llanes; Master Andrés de Larragati, surgeon of the said Armada, and Martin de Villachica, a citizen of Cadiz. And the said Pedro Menéndez de Avilés, the testator, and the said gentlemen signed it with their signatures in the register of the notary for this document, and I, the aforesaid notary, know the said testator, and signed it likewise.

Item: I say and declare that I loaned about 300 ducats, more or less, to Captain Gutierre de Solis, as is contained in a legal paper drawn up to this effect; of which 300 ducats or thereabouts, I have received nothing; I order that half of this shall be collected from the said Captain Gutierre de Solis, and

238

the other half I remit and they shall not ask it of him.

Done and executed ut supra, the aforesaid being witnesses, and it was signed by the said Pedro Menéndez Adelantado, and by the said witnesses and the present notary.

The signatures read: Pedro Menéndez, Licentiate Martin Ruiz de Olalde, Fray Juan de Madariaga, Andrés de Larraguti, Gabriel de Untoria, Martin de Villachica.--
Before me, Pedro de Ceballos.

And after the aforesaid, in the said house of Hano, on the said 15th day of the said month of September of the said year 1574, the said Señor Adelantado Pedro Menéndez, in the presence of me, the said Pedro de Ceballos, notary, and the witnesses above mentioned, said that besides and in addition to the aforesaid, he bequeathed 200 ducats to Don Balthasar de Cient Fuegos, Ensign of the Royal Standard of the aforesaid Armada, which shall be paid him from his funds. And he said likewise that he bequeathed another 200 gold ducats to Don Francisco Maldonado, brother of the said Don Diego

Maldonado; which it was his wish, and he directed, that I should hold.

Furthermore, he bequeathed 10 ducats as a donation to the Reverend Fray Juan de Madariaga, the present Superior of the Monastery of San Francisco of the town of Santander, so that he may remember in his orisons to pray to God for his soul; and the said Señor Pedro Menéndez, Adelantado, said that he executed these said bequests in the aforesaid manner; being present as witnesses to the aforesaid, Licentiate Cereceda, a physician, a citizen of Laredo; Licentiate Martin Ruiz, a physician, a citizen of Portugalete; Martin de Villachica, a follower of Don Juan Menéndez de Recalde, and the said Adelantado, the testator, whom I, the said notary, certify that I know. He signed it with his signature in the said register, and the said witnesses signed it likewise, and I, the said notary.

The signatures read: Pedro Menéndez, Cereceda, Licentiate Martin Ruiz de Olalde, Martin de Villachica--Before me, Pedro de Ceballos.

And I, the aforesaid Pedro de Ceballos, notary public for his Majesty at his court and through all his kingdoms and dominions, and for the public of the said town of Santander; who was present with the said witnesses at the execution of the said will and codicil, and everything therein set forth by the said Pedro Menéndez de Avilés, the aforesaid Adelantado, who signed his signature in the register when the said witnesses signed theirs, whom I certify that I know; had this said copy of the said will and codicil, and everything therein contained, written and copied on this sheet and half of an entire sheet of paper, and at the end of each page there is the accustomed rubric; in order to give it to the said Hernando de Miranda, an executor of the said Adelantado and his son-in-law, who asked me for this signed copy, notwithstanding that before I had given him one signed; and let it be understood that all of it, and any other copy whatever which may have been given of this will, are all one same will, as in effect it is; and at the end I signed and certified it for the said Hernando de Miranda, and I here affixed my signum.

In testimony of the truth,

Pedro de Ceballos.

The Governors of Florida

Florida's present chief executive, Claude R. Kirk, Jr., is Florida's 141st governor. Future research may reveal additions to that number.

Juan Ponce de León was Florida's first governor in residence. He discovered Florida in 1513; and in 1521, with the title of governor, he came back to settle Florida's west coast. The Indians mortally wounded him, and the colony soon dissolved.

Lucas Vásquez de Ayllón had the title in 1526-1527, and settled north of the present Georgia line but in the broad area then known as Florida. Pánfilo de Narváez, carrying the title, camped at Pensacola in 1528 in another short-lived effort. Hernando de Soto, with the title of adelantado, came in 1539 to Florida, but, admittedly, he came primarily as an explorer. Tristán de Luna y Arellano established himself as governor of Florida in a substantial settlement at Pensacola in 1559-1561.

Others had the title in these early days but did little to justify it. An excellent discussion of these matters is to be found in John Jay TePaske, *The Governorship of Spanish Florida, 1700-1763* (Durham, Duke University Press, 1964). And lists of early governors are in Kathryn Abbey Hanna, *Florida: Land of Change* (Chapel Hill, University of North Carolina Press, 1948), in Robert Ranson, *Chronology* (St. Augustine, 1930), and in a list published in 1961 by Luis R. Arana.

Jean Ribault led for France an expedition to Florida in 1562 which erected boundary markers in Florida and South Carolina. He deputized Captain Albert de la Pierria to govern in his absence at Charlesfort, a tiny settlement in present-day South Carolina. The latter was executed by members of the colony, which then chose as his successor Nicolas Barré. René de Laudonnière began the permanent settlement of Florida in 1564 with his colony, Fort Caroline; and shortly before its capture by the Spanish, Jean Ribault joined Fort Caroline as the new governor there. The conqueror was Pedro Menéndez de Avilés. The list of Florida governors from him to Melchor Feliú was taken from a list in the second volume of J. T. Connor, *Colonial Records of Spanish Florida* (DeLand, Florida State Historical Society, 1925), with several additions made up from the lists of TePaske and Arana.

The list of governors in the British and the Second Spanish Occupation is taken from Caroline M. Brevard, *A History of Florida from the Treaty of 1763 to Our Own Times* (DeLand, Florida State Historical Society, 1924), which was edited by J. H. Robertson. The list of governors for the period after the United States acquired Florida is taken from Allen Morris, *Our Florida Government* (Chicago, Lyons and Carnahan, 1961), and also from Brevard.

The seat of government for West Florida was Pensacola and that of East Florida was St. Augustine, which was also the seat of government for all Florida during the first Spanish occupation period. Tallahassee was chosen as the American territorial capital site in 1823.

It should be noted that portions of Florida have been at times under flags of occupation or of local independence and that chief officials of these small areas are not listed because they can hardly be classified as governors of Florida. Examples are the French occupation of Pensacola in the early eighteenth century, movements for separate independence in both East and West Florida, and the seizures of Fernandina by buccaneers operating under South and Central American flags. Also for brief intermittent periods during the Spanish regimes there was no one person who actually served as governor, and treasury officials acted in place of governors. Since they were not really governors they have been excluded from this list.

The Age of Discovery and Exploration

Spanish

Juan Ponce de León	1513 and 1521
Alonzo Álvarez de Piñeda	1519
Lucas Vásquez de Ayllón	1526-1527
Pánfilo de Narváez	1528
Hernando de Soto	1539
Tristán de Luna y Arellano	1559-1561
Angel de Villafañe	1563

French

Jean Ribault	1562 and 1565
Albert de la Pierria	1562
Nicolas Barré	1563
René de Laudonnière	1564-1565

The First Spanish Period

Pedro Menéndez de Avilés	1565-1574

(Acting during the frequent absences of Menéndez: Pedro Menéndez de Valdés; Esteban de las Alas; Pedro Menéndez de Avilés, the younger; Pedro Menéndez Marqués; Diego de Velasco.)

Hernando de Miranda	1576
Gutierre de Miranda	1576-1577
Pedro Menéndez Márquez, ad interim	1577-1578
Pedro Menéndez Márquez	1578-1589

(Acting during the frequent absences of Menéndez Márquez: Gutierre de Miranda; Juan de Posada.)

Gutierre de Miranda	1589-1592
Rodrigo de Junco, appointed, was drowned	1592
Francisco de Salazar	1592-1594
Domingo Martínez de Avendaño	1594-1595
Gonçalo Méndez de Canço	1596-1603
Pedro de Ybarra	1603-1609
Juan Fernández de Olivera	1609-1612
Juan de Tribiño Guillamas	1613-1618
Juan de Salinas	1618-1623
Luis de Rojas y Borja	1624-1629
Andrés Rodríguez de Villegas	1630-1631
Nicolás Ponce de León I	1631-1633
Luis Horruytiner	1633-1638
Damián de Vega Castro y Pardo	1639-1645
Benito Ruíz de Salazar Ballecilla, deposed 1646, reinstated 1647	1645-1650
Nicolás Ponce de León I	1651
Pedro Benedit Horruytiner, ad interim	1651-1654
Diego de Rebolledo	1655-1659
Alonso de Aranguiz y Cortés	1659-1663
Nicolás Ponce de León II	1663-1664
Francisco de la Guerra y de la Vega	1664-1670
Manuel de Cendoya	1670-1673
Nicolás Ponce de León II	1673-1675
Pablo de Hita Salazar	1675-1680
Juan Márquez Cabrera	1680-1687
Pedro de Aranda y Avellaneda	1687
Diego de Quiroga y Lozada	1687-1693

243

Andrae de la Páez	1693
Laureano de Torres y Ayala	1693-1699
José de Zuñiga y Cerda	1699-1706
Francisco de Córcoles y Martínez	1706-1716
Pedro de Olivera y Fullana	1716
Juan de Ayala Escobar, ad interim	1716-1718
Antonio de Benavides	1718-1727
Antonio Malini, ad interim	1719
Ignacio Rodríguez Roso	1727-1728
Antonio de Benavides	1728-1734
Francisco del Moral y Sánchez	1734-1737
Manuel José de Justis, ad interim	1737
Manuel de Montiano	1737-1749
Melchor de Navarrete	1749-1752
Fulgencio García de Solís, ad interim	1752-1755
Alonso Fernández de Heredia	1755-1758
Lucas de Palacio y Valenzuela	1758-1761
Alonso de Cárdenas, ad interim	1761-1762
Melchor Feliú	1762-1763

The English Period

East Florida

John Hedges	1763
Francis Ogilvie	1763-1764
James Grant	1764-1771
John Moultrie	1771-1774
Patrick Tonyn	1774-1783

West Florida

Augustine Prevost	1763-1764
Robert Farmer (at Mobile)	1763-1764
George Johnstone	1764-1767
Montfort Browne	1767-1769
John Eliot	1769
Montfort Browne	1769
Elias Durnford	1769-1770
Peter Chester	1770-1781

The Second Spanish Period

East Florida

Vicente Manuel de Zéspedes	1783-1790
Juan Nepomuceno de Quesada	1790-1796
Bartolomé Morales, acting	1795
José de Ortega, acting	1796
Enrique White	1796-1811
Juan José de Estrada, acting	1811-1812
Sebastián Kindelán y Oregón	1812-1815
Juan José de Estrada, acting	1815-1816
José Coppinger	1816-1821

West Florida

Esteban Miro	1781
Arturo O'Neill	1781-1793
Pedro Piernas, acting	1785
Francisco Cruzat, acting	1789

244

Jacobo Dubreuil	1789
Enrique White	1793-1795
Francisco de Paula Gelabert, acting	1796
Vicente Folch y Juan	1796-1809
Francisco Maximiliano de San Maxent	1809
Vicente Folch y Juan	1809
Francisco Maximiliano de San Maxent	1809-1810
Francisco Collell	1810-1811
Francisco Maximiliano de San Maxent	1811-1812
Mauricio de Zuñiga	1812-1813
Mateo González Manrique	1813-1815
José de Soto	1815-1816
Mauricio de Zuñiga	1816
Francisco Maximiliano de San Maxent	1816
José Masot	1816-1819
José María Callava	1819-1821

The American Period

Military

Major General Andrew Jackson	1821
Captain John R. Bell, acting, East Florida	1821
William G. D. Worthington, acting, East Florida	1821-1822
George Walton, acting, West Florida	1821-1822

Territorial

William P. DuVal	1822-1834
John H. Eaton	1834-1835
Richard Keith Call	1835-1840
Robert Raymond Reid	1840-1841
Richard Keith Call	1841-1844
John Branch	1844

State

William D. Moseley	1845-1849
Thomas Brown	1849-1853
James E. Broome	1853-1857
Madison S. Perry	1857-1861
John Milton	1861-1865
A. K. Allison, acting	1865
William Marvin, provisional, Presidential proclamation	1865
David S. Walker	1865-1868
Harrison Reed	1868-1873
Samuel T. Day, acting	1872
Ossian B. Hart	1873-1874
M. L. Stearns	1874-1877
George F. Drew	1877-1881
William D. Bloxham	1881-1885
Edward A. Perry	1885-1889
Francis P. Fleming	1889-1893
Henry L. Mitchell	1893-1897
William D. Bloxham	1897-1901
William S. Jennings	1901-1905
Napoleon B. Broward	1905-1909
Albert W. Gilchrist	1909-1913
Park Trammell	1913-1917
Sidney J. Catts	1917-1921

Cary A. Hardee	1921-1925	Fuller Warren	1949-1953
John W. Martin	1925-1929	Dan T. McCarty, died in office	1953
Doyle E. Carlton	1929-1933	Charley E. Johns, acting	1953-1955
David Sholtz	1933-1937	LeRoy Collins	1955-1961
Fred P. Cone	1937-1941	Farris Bryant	1961-1965
Spessard L. Holland	1941-1945	Haydon Burns	1965-1967
Millard F. Caldwell	1945-1949	Claude R. Kirk, Jr.	1967 ——

Annotated Index

A

Adelano: Indian chief visited by the French, 102. *See also* Edelano

Amaya, Diego de: head pilot for Menéndez and in command of a company of infantry, 154

Appalachian Mountains: source of gold, silver, and copper, 84, 95; method of mining there, 84, 85 (picture), 108; expedition for gold sent by French to this area, 99, 103; King Oustaca knew the route to the mountains, 108

Arlac, M. de: Laudonnière's ensign, 100

Athore: son of Satirioua, 18; married his mother, 18; picture, 18, 19

Audusta: Indian king in the area of Charlesfort, South Carolina, 106

Avilés, Bartolomé Menéndez de: brother of Pedro Menéndez and a naval captain at St. Augustine, 154

Avilés, Pedro Menéndez de: portrait of, iv; sent by Philip II to conquer La Caroline and to found St. Augustine, xiv; prior to settlement of La Caroline reported as opposed to settling Florida, 127; Connor's appraisal of him, 147, 186; three letters of, 147 *et seq.;* his fleet contacted the French fleet, 150; landed at St. Augustine on September 6, 1565, 150; in need of horses, 152; planned to plant grain, 155; observed gold among Indians, 155; escaped from French at St. Augustine because of shallow harbor entrance, the French urging surrender, 161; took advantage of French being at sea to march against La Caroline and capture it, 161; executed first group of Frenchmen at Matanzas, 163; executed second group of Frenchmen at Matanzas, including Ribault, 174; Knight of the Order of Santiago, 231; Adelantado of Florida, Captain General of the Armada, 231; appointed Pedro del Castillo executor of his will, 231; left bulk of estate to widow, daughter, and designated relatives, 231 *et seq.;* required certain beneficiaries under his will to take his name, 232, 233; title of Marquis, 233; placed obligation on certain beneficiaries to live in Florida for ten years, 234; codicil to will, 235; to be buried at Avilés, 236; made plea in codicil for king to pay obligations incurred on faith of royal reimbursement, 237

B

Bourdet, Captain: visited La Caroline in 1564, 129; subject of 1563 letter from Charles IX, 129

C

Calos: an Indian king of lower east coast of Florida, 104

Calos: lower east coast of Florida, 105

Cape Canaveral (Cape Kennedy): where Oathkaqua lived, 106; sighted by Menéndez on August 25, 1565, 149; under study by Menéndez for fort site, 168

Cape Florida: southeast tip of Florida, see Le Moyne map, 2, 3

Caroline, La (Fort Caroline): began the permanent settlement of what is now the U.S., xv, xvi; picture of, under construction, 20, 21; picture of, when completed, 22, 23; war in support of Outina, 32; construction of, 94; lack of food at, 95, 110; ships built in Florida for, 95, 110; omission of religious minister among original settlers at, 95; mutiny at, 100, 101, 108 et seq.; war against Outina, 110; destruction of fortifications of, 111; endangered Spain's trade routes, 125; located on bank of St. Johns River near St. Johns Bluff in present-day city limits of Jacksonville, Florida, 125; renamed San Mateo by Spanish, 158; children born at La Caroline, 163; French people who fled La Caroline and were captured but not executed numbered fifty, 163; Huguenot religious teachers at,

163; 150 French who escaped from the Spanish conquest in Florida and remained free in woods after the French ships left, 175; cruelties to the French described as having taken place at La Caroline, 203

Catherine de Medici: mother of Charles IX of France, decided that the Charlesfort and La Caroline expeditions should be undertaken, xiv; claimed Ribault had first discovered land which the French settled in Florida, 142; informed of the fall of La Caroline, 179; expressed her displeasure at the way the French were treated, 180; requested reparations for the injuries done at La Caroline, 181; was pleased at the revenge inflicted by Gourgues, 188

Charlesfort: built in 1562 by the French on present-day Parris Island, South Carolina, at Port Royal, xiv, 12, 106

Charles IX: youthful king of France, after whom Charlesfort and La Caroline were named, but his mother (Catherine) was decisive factor in the settlements being undertaken, xiv; ordered Coligny to organize La Caroline expedition to Florida, 91; wrote 1563 letter con-

cerning Captain Bourdet and the Charlesfort settlement, 129; reported as growing lusty and ready for marriage, 144; informed of the fall of La Caroline, 179; let his mother make important state decisions, 181; Catherine's opinions concerning his proposed marriage, 181, 182; died May 30, 1574, remorseful over persecution of Protestants, 197

Châtillon, Admiral de. See Coligny, Gaspard de

Coligny, Gaspard de: advised Charles IX and Catherine to sponsor La Caroline expedition to Florida, xiv, 91, 142; sent out the 1564 La Caroline expedition, 125; championed Gourgues, 188; greatly esteemed by Charles IX, 189

E

Edelano Island: 107. See also Adelano, 102

F

Ferrière, La Roche: led expedition to find gold in the Appalachian Mountains area, 99

Florida Keys: called by the Spanish and French "The Martyrs," 104; reported to be location chosen by French for the building of a fort, 166

Fort Caroline. *See* Caroline, La

Fourneaux, M. de: the leader of malcontents at La Caroline, 99, 100; returned after mutiny, 109

Fort George Island: Menéndez planned to fortify, to command the St. Johns River, 148

French Cape: where the French approached Florida near present-day St. Augustine, 4; picture of, 4, 5

French traders: Menéndez said they had a large trade in bison hides, 169

G

Gambré, Pierre: murdered by Indians, 86, 87, 103; picture of, 86, 87; traded with Indians, 86, 102; reared by Coligny, 102

Gièvre, M. de: accused Laudonnière of improprieties, 96; exiled, 97

Gold: found in Appalachian Mountains, 84, 95; method used by Indians to mine, 84, 85 (picture), 108; to be held in common for all, at La Caroline, 92, 99; provided by Outina, 98; French expedition to the Appalachian Mountains brought back gold, silver, copper, and sapphires, 101, 102; Menéndez observed gold among Indians, 155

Gourgues, Dominique de: revenged the fall of La Caroline, xv, 187; born in 1530, 186; fought in Italy, 186; captured by Spanish to become a chained Spanish galley slave, 186; captured by Turks to continue as galley slave and finally freed by another capture, 186; served the Guises, 186; a Catholic, 186; after revenge expedition lived for a while in hiding with a price on his head, 189; participated in siege of La Rochelle, 193; refused to obey orders to fall back before English squadron at La Rochelle, 195; ordered to Poland, 196; died in 1582 on his way to fight Spain for Portugal, 197; his will providing for his natural daughter Claude, 198; undertook the expedition to Florida because others would not, 204

Gourgues expedition to Florida: 1567-1568 voyage of revenge to Florida headed by Dominique de Gourgues, xv, 187; picture of battle of, 184; embarked from Bordeaux on August 2, 1567, 204; type of arms provided for expedition, 205; finally sailed on August 22, 1567, 205; fought Negroes in Africa, 205; mission revealed to men only after arrival in New World, 208; welcomed and assisted by Indians, 209, 211; recovered a French youth, 211, 213; two new forts at the mouth of the St. Johns River confronted the expedition, 218; attack on first fort, 217; attack on second fort, 218; capture of Spanish spy from San Mateo, 219; Gourgues approached Fort San Mateo from St. Johns Bluff, 220; attack on San Mateo, 220; captured Spaniards hung, 221, 222; the three forts destroyed, 222; left Florida on May 3, 1568, 224; arrived at La Rochelle on June 6, 1568, 224

H

Havre-de-Grâce: embarkation point for La Caroline expedition, 92

Hawkins, John: English navigator who visited and aided La Caroline, 110 *et seq.*, 136, 139, 140

Hayes, Jean des: chief artificer at La Caroline, 95; built ships in Florida for La Caroline, 95

Huguenot religion: the faith of many of the French settlers, xiii, 95, 125

I

Indians: in Florida at time of first settlements, pictures of, 4 through 9, 12, 13, 16 through 87; method of combat, preparations for combat and victory celebrations, 24 through 35, 64, 65, 68, 69; hermaphrodites among them and assigned duties of same, 36, 37, 60, 61 (including pictures); mourning ceremonies, 38 through 41; use of tobacco, 42, 43; care of sick, 42, 43; agriculture, 44, 45; granaries, 46, 47; gathering stores, 48, 49; food preparation, 50, 51; hunting deer, 52, 53; killing alligators, 54, 55; swimming, 56, 57; feast preparations, 58, 59; ceremonial activities, 60, 61; fortifications, 62, 63; spent part of each year in woods, 62; punishment among, 66, 67; human sacrifice, 70, 71; stag ceremony, 72, 73; amusements, 74, 75; betrothal ceremonies for king's bride, 76 through 79; dress of, 78, 93; tattooed, 80, 81; foodstuffs of, 92; ceremonies at death of king or priest, 82, 83; mining methods, 84, 85; musicians among, 94; at La Caroline friendly to the French, 94; their name for enemy: "Timogua", 102; at St. Augustine friendly to the Spanish, 151; killed some Spaniards, 156; their religion described by Menéndez, 157; Spanish soldiers taught religion to them, 157; priests needed among them, 158; taught the reformed religion by the French, 163; assisted Gourgues expedition, 209, 211

J

Jean, François: a mutineer who led the Spanish to La Caroline, 114; visited on ship of Jacques Ribault, 117
Jesuits: letter of Menéndez to a Jesuit friend, 156

L

La Caille, Captain: assigned to meet Saturioua, 24, 93; reported dissension to Laudonnière, 97; loyal to Laudonnière, 100; fled to woods during onset of mutiny, 100, 103; captured mutineers, 109; envoy with Nicolas Verdier to Menéndez at Matanzas, 119
La Croix: a leader of malcontents at La Caroline, 99; returned to La Caroline after mutiny, 109
Lake Okeechobee: possibly Lake Sarrope in Le Moyne's map and text, 105. The only other possibility is Lake George
Laudonnière, René de: appointed head of La Caroline expedition, xiv, 18, 91; picture of, 18, 19; rejected plea of Saturioua to assist in war, 96; rejected plea of French mutineers for expedition to New Spain, 98; plot to kill him, 100; captured by his own men, 100; forced to sign document requesting supplies in New Spain, 101; reorganized his troops after mutiny, 103; governed La Caroline settlement, 125; escaped from La Caroline massacre, 162; hit by pike blow, 162; his voyage of 1572, 193.
Le Moyne de Morgues, Jacques: official cartographer and artist of the La Caroline expedition, 2; map and drawings, 2 through 87; was one of those sent out under Ottigny to assist Outina in combat, 32; was on expedition that captured Outina,

68; his narrative, 89 through 122; sent back from Ribault's fleet to La Caroline on account of convalescent condition, 114; escaped fort to return to Europe, xv, 115

M

Martínez, Father: murdered by Indians, 158; notes, 160

Martyrs: early name for the Florida Keys, 104, 166

Matanzas Inlet: where on September 29, 1565, some of Ribault's forces were slain by Menéndez, with some 16 being spared death, 164; where Ribault and his followers were executed on October 12, 1565, sparing five lives, 174

Mayport: where the French erected a monument in 1562, 18; picture of monument, 18, 19

Menéndez. *See* Avilés

Mutiny at La Caroline: 99 *et seq.*, 108 *et seq.;* some mutineers were hanged in Jamaica, 136; Hawkins said he saw four of them who had been hanged at La Caroline, 141

O

Outina: Indian king, enemy of Saturioua, and through whose lands lay the path to the gold and silver mines of the Appalachian Mountains, 26, 95; assisted by the French in combat against Potanou, 26 through 29; pictures of, 26 through 35; captured by the French as hostage for the provision of foodstuffs, 68, 110

Ottigny, M. d': Laudonnière's lieutenant, 26; assisted Outina in combat, 26, 28; second in command to Laudonnière, 93; assigned to meet Saturioua, 93; executed by Spanish, 120

P

Pearls: furnished to French by Outina, 99

Philip II: Spanish king, ordered on September 23, 1561, that consideration be given as to whether future settlements in Florida should be abandoned, xiii, 125, 126, 127; sent Menéndez to conquer La Caroline, xiv; Catherine complains to, about La Caroline's fall, 181

Port Royal: location of Parris Island in present-day South Carolina where Charlesfort was built in 1562, xiv, 106; picture of, 12, 13

R

Revilla Gigedo, Conde de: owner of Menéndez portrait, descendant of Menéndez, and Spanish titular Governor of Florida, iv

Ribaud, Jacques. *See* Ribault, Jacques

Ribaud, Jean. *See* Ribault, Jean

Ribault Bay: left water entrance shown in Le Moyne's picture of River of May and now the berthing basin for Navy carriers at the Mayport Naval Station at Jacksonville, Florida, 6, 7 (picture)

Ribault, Jacques: son of Jean Ribault, 111; was in command of one of three small ships in St. Johns River at the time of fall of La Caroline, 117; his ship visited by traitor François Jean, 117

Ribault, Jean: explored Florida and left a colony at Charlesfort, South Carolina in 1562, xiv, 91, 135, 203; Menéndez praised him, 174; came to La Caroline to succeed Laudonnière, xv, 111; decided to attack the Spanish at sea, 113;

was shipwrecked with his men, 114; executed by the Spanish on October 12, 1565, 120, 174; had planned an expedition to America in 1563 with Thomas Stukeley, under English patronage, 131; was captured and imprisoned in England in 1563, 133

River of Dolphins: site of St. Augustine visited by the Charlesfort and La Caroline expeditions, 4; named by Laudonnière, 4; picture of, 4, 5

River of May. *See* St. Johns River

Roussi: a French lad left behind from the 1562 Charlesfort expedition, 106; sought by Laudonnière, 106; captured by Spanish, 107

S

St. Augustine, Florida: why established by Spanish, xiv, 125; the oldest settlement by Europeans within present U.S., xiv, 125; reconnoitered by Menéndez on St. Augustine's Day, 1565, 150; soldiers landed there on September 6, 1565, 150; married men with wives and children put on shore on September 7, 1565, 150; Menéndez landed September 8, 1565,

150; approached by French fleet September 8, 1565, 150; in need of horses, 152; lack of food at, 156, 175; seventeen ships visit, 156; requested financial assistance, 170, 172

St. Johns Bluff: a 70-foot-high and heavily wooded sand bluff on the south side of the St. Johns River adjacent to the site of La Caroline and called by the French a mountain, 20, 220

St. Johns River: called by the French "River of May," 6, 92; picture of, 6, 7; La Caroline site, 20, 203; reached by the La Caroline expedition on June 22, 1564, 92; reached by Spanish fleet on September 4, 1565, 149; believed by Menéndez to have an opening on the Gulf of Mexico, 167, 171

San Mateo: visited by a boat from the ship from which Father Martínez landed, 158; was what the Spanish renamed La Caroline, 167, 171; located at 30.25 degrees, 168; burned, 173

San Vicente, Captain Juan: one of leaders in the first Spanish landing at St. Augustine, 153

Sapphires: brought back to La Caroline from Appalachian expedition, 102

Saturioua (Saturiba): picture of, 24, 25; Indian king in whose lands La Caroline was settled, 24, 93; ordered his men to help build La Caroline, 94; assisted Gourgues, 209, 211

Settlements in Florida: by Europeans before permanent settlements of 1564-1565, xi *et seq.*, 241 *et seq.*

Ships at La Caroline: *Elizabeth of Honfleur,* 92; ship under Captain Pierre, 96; Hawkins' ship, 110; *the Pearl,* 111; *the Trinity,* 112; the Spanish fleet, 149

Spanish ambassadors, letters of, to Philip II: from Bishop Alvero de la Quadra, May 1, 1563, 131; *id.,* June 19, 1563, 132, 133; June 26, 1563, 134, 135; from Guzmán de Silva, October 1, 1565, 136; *id.,* October 8, 1565, 137; *id.,* October 22, 1565, 138, 139; *id.,* November 5, 1565, 140, 141; April 6, 1566, 142, 143; May 18, 1566, 144, 145

Stephen: an Italian and a leader of malcontents at La Caroline, 99; returned to La Caroline after mutiny, 109

Stukeley, Thomas: planned an English-sponsored expedition with Jean Ribault to America, 131; reported as wishing to serve Philip II, 137; reported as planning to bore holes in the Ribault ships so the men would perish and the English plan would fail, xiv, 138

T

Timucuan Indians: Indian word "Timogua" meant enemy, 102. *See also* Indians

Tobacco: 42, 43

Trenchant: forced to pilot a ship of mutineers from La Caroline, 101; returned to La Caroline with mutineers, 109

V

Valdés, Diego Florez de: admiral of the fleet of Menéndez, 154; sent to Havana, 154; sent by Menéndez to Spain, 173; Menéndez sought knighthood and aid for, 173

Valdés, Pedro Menéndez de: appointed as lieutenant to Menéndez and camp master at St. Augustine, 153

Vasseur, Michael le: royal navigator sent on La Caroline expedition, 91; forced to pilot a ship of mutineers from La Caroline, 101

Vasseur, Thomas le: royal navigator sent on La Caroline expedition, 91; went to the area of Charlesfort to search for Roussi, 106; sent by Ribault while at Matanzas to see how things went at La Caroline, 119

Vigne, M. de la: officer of the guard when La Caroline was attacked, 114

Villarroel, Gonzalo de: appointed as sergeant major to Menéndez, 153